# THE SOUND OF MUSICALS

Ruth Leon

# The Sound
# Of Musicals

OBERON BOOKS

LONDON

First published in 2010 by Oberon Books Ltd
521 Caledonian Road, London N7 9RH
Tel: 020 7607 3637 / Fax: 020 7607 3629
e-mail: info@oberonbooks.com
www.oberonbooks.com

A catalogue record for this book is available from the
British Library.

ISBN: 978-1-84943-018-0

Printed in Great Britain by CPI Antony Rowe, Chippenham

# Contents

# Why Musicals?

EVERYBODY SINGS. THE first sounds made by a human baby more closely resemble music than speech. A toddler will sing before he speaks. He hears music before he recognizes words.

Dancing is natural. Without volition, the body moves to musical stimulus. Hear a rhythm, sway or stamp or jiggle.

Telling stories is the way we communicate. Even a simple greeting – "Good morning" – is the beginning of a story, a narrative where we tell each other about ourselves.

So what is a musical? It's simply a way to combine the most basic of our human actions. Speech, music, song, dance, when organized, become a multi-faceted artistic expression which, in any combination or society, is just the highest form of story-telling.

Think of an African ritual. The dancers stamp and turn while drummers beat out the rhythm and the singers, often the dancers, tell a story. American Indians sing and dance their religion, their songs asking for rain or good crops, telling of their ancestors. Shinto priests combine their movements with their chants as do Buddhist monks, while Jewish rites all involve movement and song. Even Muslims, for whom song and dance are forbidden in religious ritual, sing their calls to prayer and move in unison on their prayer mats. Yes, there are Christian sects such as the Amish, which deny themselves music and dance, but most revel in the singing of hymns and what are they but songs which tell a story? The combination of song, dance, speech and music, is practically universal and almost as basic to human life as food and shelter.

All peoples communicate. With the gift of language comes the creative need to go beyond words. My cat may clearly indicate that he likes Kern and hates Wagner by either stretching and purring or by covering his pointy ears with his paw but he doesn't try to sing along or dance to either. If you discount birds and whales, for whom song is their form of language, we can safely assume that only humans sing and dance. And we do so, not because we have decided to but because we can't help ourselves.

Once you accept that combining speech, music, song, and dance is not, as others have claimed, an artifice imposed by an elite but a basic human need, you can go on to ask the basic question: how did we get from the simplicity of a prayer expressed in simple movement to a modern day musical? A big musical has dozens of people onstage and at least an equal number backstage. How did we develop the need for stars, supporting artistes, chorus girls and boys (they're always 'girls' and 'boys' even if they're collecting their pensions), a pit orchestra, a sound crew, a lighting gang, dressers, stage and company managers, publicists, and the whole paraphernalia of a stage show?

Just lucky, I guess.

And before that lot ever get that far, there are the 'creatives'. There's a composer, a lyricist, a book writer, a director, set, costume, sound, and lighting designers, a choreographer, an arranger, a casting director, a conductor, and about a dozen more in support of them. Oh, and a producer, the man or woman who gets them all together and raises the money, often a not inconsiderable task with Broadway musicals costing millions. Often, these days, the money is so enormous that there has to be more than one producer. Sometimes there are so many of them bunched above the show's title that they outnumber the cast.

And what they all have in common is belief. It's like a little religion. They believe in what they're doing, believe they are breaking new ground, believe they have the best-ever team, believe that it will succeed, believe that the audience will applaud and tell their friends, believe that the critics will like it and tell their readers, believe that they are, collectively, making the best show in the world or, at least, the best show on Broadway or in the West End, this season. Unless everybody involved believes this, their show, no matter how well meant, will fail. And, often, it will fail even if they do believe.

Everybody who works in the theatre will at some point refer to the team on the show they are doing or have just done as a family. This is particularly true of musicals. Mounting a major musical is such a monumental task and involves so many people over such a long but concentrated period of time that the outside world ceases to have meaning for them. Members of the cast and crew become so close after weeks of being together all the time that they will forget the birthdays of their children, come home late or not at all, fall in love with their co-star to whom in other circumstances they would have nothing to say, become embroiled in the intricacies of the show to the extent of being unaware of massive world events, and create a private universe in which they are the only inhabitants.

A play is a conversation between the actors, the director and, most importantly, the playwright. There are only the words and what they do with them. Across 400 years Shakespeare continues an ongoing dialogue with those who perform his plays and can tell them, if they will listen, exactly what he wants from them.

Musicals are different. They can be driven by a variety of different engines and the performers must adjust with each show to whichever engine drives that particular production. Say *West Side Story* to almost anyone and chances are their first instinct is to mention Jerome Robbins' ground-breaking dances in the fight between the Jets and the Sharks. So 'dance' is the engine that drives *West Side Story* but it is Shaw's *Pygmalion*, the play on which it is based, that underpins everything in *My Fair Lady*. Words is the engine here, not movement. Character motivates *Gypsy*, the character of Mama Rose, and Jerome Kern's melodies animate *Showboat* and, it could be argued, that Oscar Hammerstein's lyrics are the bedrock of *South Pacific*. Each great musical has its own vocabulary and syntax and what defines it can only be determined after it has come together.

A great musical then is one which is organic, which grows out of its material, where every element is designed to strengthen the same ends and in which the ends not only justify the means but *are* the means. Where song, dance, speech and movement are indivisible and where the whole enterprise entertains, informs and amazes you.

When you've got all that, though, there's still another indefinable element. Some call it stage magic. It is the charisma that lifts it above all the others and makes it transcendent. If you've got that, along with all the rest, you've got a perfect musical. It's happened maybe five, maybe ten, all right, maybe fifteen times in human history. Easy. Even a baby can do it.

# 1. Something Wonderful

ASK HALF A dozen lovers of the musical what are the five best musicals ever and the answers will come back fast. The first three are easy. *West Side Story, My Fair Lady, Guys and Dolls.* Almost everybody agrees on them. Where opinions start to diverge is on the other two. *Oklahoma!, Gypsy, Showboat,* are all contenders as are *Sweeney Todd, Fiddler on the Roof, Sunday in the Park with George* and *South Pacific.* And we've barely scratched the surface, not of musicals but of great musicals.

Add to these the other major works by composers and lyricists already on the list – Bernstein, Lerner and Loewe, Frank Loesser, Rodgers and Hart, Rodgers and Hammerstein, Porter, Sondheim, Jule Styne, Lionel Bart, Bock and Harnick, Kern – and think of all the great musicals written by those who aren't on the list. Then you begin to see the magnitude of the argument.

Friends have been known to stop speaking because they couldn't bear to leave their own particular favourite off the list, "What? Can I believe my ears? You are not including anything by George Gershwin (or Johnny Mercer or Yip Harburg or Harold Arlen or any of almost countless others)?" Men have come to blows for less.

So. Given the seriousness of the subject, perhaps we should look at what makes a perfect musical. Sheridan Morley, the great English drama critic, used to say that a great musical was at least as good as a great play and he would equate Stephen Sondheim's *Company*, a favourite show of his, with *King Lear*. Douglas Hodge, the actor who took the title role in Shakespeare's *Titus Andronicus* and then played Zaza, the drag queen in the triumphant production of *La Cage aux Folles* which transferred from the West End to Broadway agrees, "If anything, musicals require more of the actor – more energy, more concentration – because there are so many elements to consider, all the same ones you have in a play and the extras that come with music, dancing and staging."

A great musical is one in which every element of the show contributes to the whole and where the whole is indivisible. There can be no bad songs, no songs which do not drive the action of the show forward or emphasise mood, plot or character. The book, or script, has to be tight with no redundant lines. While it has to leave room for the songs, they must grow naturally out of the book, neither holding up the action nor repeating what has been said in words. The book and songs need to be so closely related that the audience is scarcely aware when spoken dialogue turns to song.

Any live stage show stands or falls by its characters and their complexity is what gets us through to the end. The audience need not love them but they have to be able to empathise with them. Some terrific shows have faltered because their leading characters were unsympathetic or the audience didn't take to them. While Henry Higgins in *My Fair Lady* is crusty and irascible, he is also lovable and the audience roots for him but Franklin Shepard in Sondheim's *Merrily We Roll Along* and Joey Evans in Rodgers and Hart's *Pal Joey* are anti-heroes whom the audience instinctively mistrusts. Only the songs can put things right when the book doesn't help.

Design plays an important part in a musical's success. Who can ever forget Cecil Beaton's black and white Ascot scene in *My Fair Lady*? It was so much more than beautiful; it stretched the imagination and aspirations of the audience who didn't just want to look at the stage, they wanted to be on it. Or Boris Aronson's evocation of a *shtetl* in *Fiddler on the Roof.* It didn't just look like a Chagall painting come to life, it was the visual image of an entire culture.

And the things you don't see or see only in passing matter just as much. Agnes de Mille virtually invented show chore-ography with her work on *Oklahoma!* where she made men simulate the gait of galloping horses and dancers fly through a dream. These dances created an indelible impression, an atmosphere which gave credibility to the entire show, even when the actors weren't dancing. It can change mood, suggest violence – think of what Jerome Robbins was able to do with 'The Rumble' in *West Side Story* – and make us want to get up and join the dancers on the stage.

Lighting too contributes hugely to the 'feel' of a show as, increasingly, does sound. You may not notice when there is a slight echo on a singer's voice or when he looks cold onstage but that is the effect of careful plotting from both sound and lighting designers. Today, sound engineers are able to accomplish remarkable feats; in the recent Broadway presentation *Come Fly Away*, they not only stripped off the strings from the original recordings of Frank Sinatra but also his voice. They were then combined with an onstage orchestra of brass and percussion so that it was as though the long-dead Sinatra was singing with a live band.

The music arranger, the person who decides what should be sung, what should be played in which key by which instrument, can centrally affect the way a musical sounds and even looks. What he hands over to the Musical Director, the conductor who is actually going to lead the orchestra in performance, will determine how many musicians will play the show, what instrumentation they will play, and how the singers will tackle the music. The stage manager, who will 'call' the show, give the cues to cast and crew, must have split-second timing and a steady nerve. Lots of things can go wrong during a show – a zipper may get stuck, a light may blow out, a piece of the technology may fail to function and it is the stage manager's job to get the show back on track fast enough that the audience never notices.

Every one of these professionals is absolutely vital to a show but sometimes, even when everything works as it should, the show itself fails to ignite. Why? Nobody knows. If they did, every musical would be perfect. As it is, what we know is that there are only five perfect musicals and, up until now, I have failed to find any sort of consensus about which they are.

*My Fair Lady, West Side Story* and *Guys and Dolls* are pretty good contenders, though. Each of these shows, and the others I have picked out of the dozens which my friends suggested should be part of this book, is here because it changed the nature and direction of the musical theatre. At the same time, each worked on its own as entertainment. To put it even more simply, people love them, but it isn't just affection that keeps the perfect musicals alive. Often unbeknown to their own creators, they each have a deeper and more significant purpose, one that connects them to the society from which they came, the audiences who are still enthusiastic about seeing them again, and the future theatregoers who don't know yet what a treat they still have in store.

I have a theory that successful theatre is where every member of the audience silently says, "me too" at some point before the final curtain. Live theatre is about us, the audience, if it works, and only about the playwright or composer, if it doesn't.

Every show in this brief set of essays is here for the same two reasons:

They have each changed the way we think about the musical theatre – its shape, its content, its scope, its direction. It is not enough to have produced a popular show – *Phantom of the Opera* and *Les Misérables* spring to mind – they must also have changed the shows that came after them and the way we, as an audience, view the future of the musical theatre.

The other essential element is the 'me too' factor. Each musical here must be, in some way, universal, speaking to something deep within each member of the audience so that each of us recognises that this show, no matter what its specific details, is about us.

Only when both these criteria are met does it then qualify as The Perfect Musical. And sometimes not even then.

# 2. Only Make Believe

IN THE SUMMER of 1928, a fire broke out in the hold of *The James Adams Floating Theatre* and the boat sank to the bottom of the Pamlico River in North Carolina. This sad accident would not need to concern us at all except that the *James Adams* had been the inspiration for the *Cotton Blossom*, the fictional vessel in Edna Ferber's novel *Showboat*, on which Jerome Kern and Oscar Hammerstein II based their groundbreaking 1927 musical.

Ferber was fascinated by the notion of a theatrical troupe that lived and worked together on a floating barge, performing their melodramas and comedies up and down the Mississippi River. Their boat was both their theatre and their home and Ferber spent a happy summer travelling from town to town on the *James Adams*. Research completed, she repaired to a quiet Basque town and wrote her book, creating unforgettable characters out of the actors, riverboat gamblers, law enforcement officers, and show people she met along the way and producing a sprawling saga, spanning many locations and five decades, through dozens of characters and many sub-plots. Her drama was gleaned from the love affairs and intrigues she encountered among people living in such close quarters and from the fallout from the race laws in the American South which allowed blacks and whites to live and work in close proximity but not to mix in any meaningful way. Ferber's novel is a wide-ranging epic, a portrait of a particular American society at a particular time in its history. Across this boundless landscape, the show-boat plies its theatrical craft.

Jerome Kern read the novel, loved it, decided it could be adapted for the stage and begged the critic, Alexander Woollcott, to introduce him to Edna Ferber. Completely by accident, on the very evening that Woollcott wrote his letter of introduction, all three – Woollcott, Kern and Ferber – went to the same theatre opening, *Criss Cross,* and the introduction was made. And, in a true sense, this is where it all began. *Showboat* wasn't, of course, the first musical ever. There had been operettas and vaudeville, music hall and plays with songs long before that dating back to *The Black Crook* in 1866 and continuing with Kern's own Princess Theatre shows in the teens, written with P.G. Wodehouse and Guy Bolton, and Florenz Ziegfeld's *Follies* in the twenties, and fluffy song-and-dance shows, but *Showboat,* in 1927, was the first ever 'book' musical, the first to deal with serious issues, the first to be more than a 'boy-meets-girl, boy-loses-girl, boy-gets-girl' evening in which short dialogue scenes were simply designed to connect the songs, jokes, girls, and dances which were their real point.

*Showboat* was different. Although Hammerstein, who wrote the libretto, had to shorten Ferber's timespan to include only the period from 1890 to the present day, that is, 1927, he retained Ferber's concerns with such subjects as slavery and miscegenation, compulsive gambling, family abandonment, drunkenness and the relative positions of black and white Americans. Even the author herself thought the enterprise was doomed. But, as it took shape, the innovative content of the novel dictated the form of the show and, by retaining several threads of the story, just as in the book, the audience would come to care about the principal characters.

The showboat is owned by the easy-going Cap'n Andy and his sharp-tongued wife, Parthenia, who, having married beneath her station, looks down on the actors and is intent on raising her daughter as a lady. But Magnolia has other ideas. Only 16 and naïve when we first meet her, Magnolia is already an accomplished singer and musician and, in an emergency, can perform onstage, much to Parthy's fury and Cap'n Andy's delight. Julie and Steve are a married couple who are the troupe's leading actors, until a jealous suitor reveals to the local sherriff that Julie is part Negro. The main plot tells the love story of Magnolia and Gaylord Ravenal ("of the Tennessee Ravenals"), a riverboat gambler, their travels and their travails. There is a comic, a villain, and a song-and-dance couple and each has their own storyline. Queenie is their cook, married to Joe, a stevedore on the Natchez levée, who sings of the mighty Mississippi and how the river doesn't care about the petty problems of those on its banks, it just keeps rolling along.

The songs by Kern and Hammerstein, far from being the purpose of the show, were there to press forward the plot, to elucidate the characters, and to indicate for the audience just when the year and setting changed. Until now, in musical theatre, songs had been their own excuse for existence and the rest of the show was always subservient to the performance of the songs. Here, Kern and Hammerstein give us cakewalk, then ragtime then jazz, which was bang up to date in 1927, in addition to the timeless love songs and classic ballads that are still part of every cabaret artist's repertoire. And the song that drives the whole show, that is emblematic of its dual themes of tradition and change, is 'Ol' Man River', in itself a most unusual musical construction, rejecting the standard 32-bar show song and bearing a Hammerstein lyric that contains only a single rhyme.

In *Showboat* it is the drama that drives the songs, not the other way around. Early in the casting process, Oscar Hammerstein, hearing Kern's melody for 'Only Make Believe' for the first time, realised that it was set very high in the soprano range. "What if," he asked, "we find a Magnolia who can't sing it?" "Then," came the uncompromising reply, "we'll find a Magnolia who can." This set the tone for the first production.

With two exceptions, every role was cast with the producer, Florenz Ziegfeld's, first choices. Those two were Harry Fender, Ziegfeld's pick for Ravenal, who suffered so severely with stagefright that he begged off, giving up the stage to become a policeman, and the great Paul Robeson, for whom the role of Joe had been created, who was unable to get out of a pre-contracted tour in time for the opening of *Showboat*. He did, however, create the role in London at the Theatre Royal, Drury Lane, the following year. Elizabeth Hines, a famous soprano, did accept the role of Magnolia but when Ziegfeld attempted to release her because *Showboat* wasn't completed by the opening date he had promised her, instead of waiting until the show was ready, she tried to sue him for breach of contract. The lawsuit went all the way to the Supreme Court and she lost but by this time had accepted another role in a far inferior show. Norma Terris got the part and the stardom that she gained from creating Magnolia still echoes down to our own time, at least in part because Magnolia was the first character in a musical to grow up, develop, and change during the course of an evening.

The rest of the cast are barely known to us today, although they were all famous in 1927. Helen Morgan, the legendary singer who sang 'Bill' was, although in her twenties, already addicted to alcohol, which lent her performance as Julie an additional note of melancholy, and Jules Bledsoe, a great operatic baritone in his time, who played Joe, died of a cerebral hemorrhage at the age of 46. Edna May Oliver, a tempestuous if horse-faced Parthy, was one of the major stage actresses of her day and Charles Winninger was a famous comic whose signature role Cap'n Andy became. Magnolia went to Norma

Terris and, in the event, Howard Marsh was the first Ravenal. Sammy White and his wife, Eva Puck, were the song-and-dance couple in the show and, of course, on the showboat. The crucial role of Queenie went to Tess Gardella, not black at all but Italian-American and, in a sign of the times, identified in the playbill only as "Aunt Jemima".

One of the major innovations was the choreography. Sammy Lee's dances departed radically from the conventions of shows of the time, the endless succession of chorus numbers and specialty scenes. His dances grew out of the story and were organically part of the show, moving comfortably through the various eras covered by the plot and the music, finding a different dance vocabulary for each number and marshalling the enormous chorus – there was a black chorus and a white chorus – into period and modern dances. From the Negro shuffle dance, through the cakewalk, ragtime and formal steps that rightly belonged to the ladies and gentlemen of Natchez to the native black African movement of 'From Dahomey', Lee's dances broke new ground.

Once again travelling first-class, Ziegfeld turned to Joseph Urban for the designs and the surviving drawings of his original sets are masterpieces of art, engineering, and ingenuity in their own right. He had, over 17 scenes, to create, among other practical sets, the Natchez levée of the Mississippi River, a grand Chicago hotel, the interior and exterior of the showboat itself, a church, a nightclub, and a boarding house, not to mention numerous back- and front-cloths so the scenery could be changed behind them. Florenz Ziegfeld, known for his girly shows and vaudeville variety, was nonetheless a producer in possession of taste, charm, and a great deal of money and he knew how to use them. He had a passion for *Showboat* and gambled his considerable theatrical know-how and business acumen on its success.

On its pre-Broadway opening night in Washington DC, it had a cast of 145 including 15 principals, and a score which, although it seems seamless to us now, consisted of specially written numbers in styles ranging across the preceding 30 years, soaring lovesongs, and interpolated numbers from the traditional 'After The Ball' to Kern's own 'Why Do I Love You?', now a classic, which was added on the road in Philadelphia. The team went on working through the pre-Broadway runs in Washington DC, Pittsburgh, Cleveland, and Philadelphia, putting in new songs, taking out dances and 'business', and generally tightening up the show, despite enthusiastic reviews and sell-out houses wherever it played. But Ziegfeld was a wily producer and he knew that the reviews that mattered would come from the New York critics and the Manhattan theatre audiences and was determined that the show would be as polished and honed as the cast and production team could make it before what turned into a historic opening night on Tuesday, December 27th, 1927.

As sometimes happens today, there were two major openings that night, *Showboat* and a new play by the author of *Philadelphia Story*, Philip Barry, so many of the critics chose the play over the musical including the most important of them all, Brooks Atkinson of the *New York Times*. He didn't get around to *Showboat* until January 6th but then was fullsome in his admiration:

> *Showboat* becomes one of those epochal works about which garrulous old men gabble for twenty-five years after the scenery has rattled off to the storehouse.

He praised every one of the principals and then gave the show his highest encomium, that this musical was as good as a straight play:

> They blend into the sort of joined, harmonised performance that we extravagantly commend in good dramatic productions.

*Showboat* would have been a monumental achievement in any era; in 1927 it was a miracle. It turned the conventional view of musical theatre on its head. Suddenly there was a musical show which was led by its drama. All its elements – music, lyrics, dance, dialogue, characters, designs – were bent to the service of its story and its creators jettisoned anything that deviated from that ambition. From that moment on, you produced a musical comedy where a silly story was a mere excuse for the songs, dances and jokes, at your peril. There were, in fact, many of these to follow but none has ever been revived, although some of their songs are still sung. *Showboat,* on the other hand, has had six major Broadway revivals since its premiere, has been filmed three times, has been produced all over the world, and is performed regularly by professionals and amateur dramatic societies alike.

One footnote: that season, the 1927-28 Broadway season, there were 264 openings. In 2010-11 there will be barely enough to reach double figures. And none of them, we can comfortably predict, will begin to approach the artistry and craft of *Showboat* which, unlike its inspiration, the *James Adams Floating Theatre*, will never sink.

## 3. Oh, What A Beautiful Mornin'

I T BEGINS, NOT with a big chorus or a stageful of singers and dancers, but with an old woman sitting alone, churning butter. From offstage we hear a voice. "Oh, what a beautiful mornin'," he sings, "Oh, what a beautiful day," and audiences in March 1943 knew they were seeing and hearing something quite different from anything they had seen or heard before. For this is *Oklahoma!*, the first, and in some ways the greatest, collaboration between the two men who wrote the seminal musicals of the twentieth century – Richard Rodgers and Oscar Hammerstein II.

They were not natural partners nor even particularly close friends. Rodgers's music had for years been accompanied by the lyrics of the friend of his youth, the troubled but much loved Lorenz Hart. Hammerstein, although responsible for the lyrics and libretti of some of the century's most successful musicals, including *Showboat* in 1927, seemed to have his good years behind him, having in recent years had a string of flops and near-misses. Not exactly a has-been, few expected him to last as the new partner of the composer with a string of recent hits to his credit, Richard Rodgers.

But Hart, plagued by illness, no longer interested in working, and increasingly addicted to alcohol, was becoming more and more unreliable so, reluctantly, Rodgers, who liked nothing so well as work, looked for a new lyricist. More than that, he needed a librettist, someone who could shape and formulate the story and characters of the shows as well as produce strong and literate lyrics. Given this job description, there weren't many candidates. Initially, Hammerstein, a thoroughly honourable man, was reluctant to step in if there was any chance that he was actually displacing Larry Hart whom he respected tremendously but he was persuaded that the brilliant Hart was, in fact, a spent force and he agreed to try working with Rodgers as they had, briefly, some years earlier. In the event, Hart died only 8 months after *Oklahoma!*'s triumphant opening night.

In 1942, in the middle of a World War, Lynn Riggs' play, *Green Grow The Lilacs,* seemed an unlikely vehicle for adaptation into a musical. It was suggested to Rodgers by Theresa Helburn of the Theatre Guild, a wily and experienced producer, who had enjoyed an out-of-town production of the play which had interpolated some traditional American folksongs into it and she reasoned that an original score would do much to improve this rural story of farmers and ranchers who wanted to turn their wild west territory into the State of Oklahoma. Rodgers was intrigued, Larry Hart flatly refused to have anything to do with it.

The subject matter and characters – simple folk on the outer fringes of the United States – were, on the face of it, antithetical to the sophistication of the Broadway musical form. These were no city slickers laughing at country bumpkins, but the settlers themselves setting out their bid to become productive members of the dominant culture, to give up their frontier justice and local lawlessness in favour of joining the system of the larger society, of becoming Americans in the true sense of belonging to a wider understanding of citizenship. *Oklahoma!* appears to be about whether Curly or Jud is going to take Laurey to the picnic but that's just what happens. What it's really about is what it means to be American, what the poet Carl Sandburg called, "the smell of new-mown hay on barn-dance floors." For soldiers serving overseas, involved in a war few of them understood, this was what they were fighting for, this was home, this was America, even if it was an America which had never really existed.

Laurey and her Aunt Eller run a small farm on the outskirts of an imaginary town called Claremore in 1906. Both Curly, a happy-go-lucky cowboy and Jud, a farmhand, are in love with Laurey and the plot turns on the rivalry between the two men and Laurey's conflict in choosing between them. The second-ary couple (almost all musicals of the era had two couples), Will Parker and flirtatious Ado Annie, have their own comic plotlines involving a shotgun wedding and a Persian peddler, but there's never any doubt about their outcomes. That's it, really, for plot. Except that after the wedding (if you don't know the plot after 75 years, I won't spoil it for you by saying who chooses whom) the emphasis is on a fire and on state-hood.

Because the producers, The Theatre Guild, had fallen on hard times, they agreed to turn over control of the production to Rodgers and Hammerstein and, consequently, there was little or no producorial interference as they set about structuring their show in a way not attempted since Gilbert and Sullivan. Hammerstein utilised much of Riggs' play, often taking a dialogue line and turning it into a lyric. Unlike his previous work with composers Jerome Kern and others where he had written his lyrics to their melodies, for *Oklahoma!* (or, as it was first titled, *Away We Go*) he wrote the libretto and lyrics together for Rodgers to set. This gave the score and book a remarkable unity, where the spoken dialogue blended seamlessly into the songs and the dances, by the ballet choreographer Agnes de Mille in her first Broadway show, were all of a piece. Stylistically, *Oklahoma!* was a single entity and the previous stop-start conventions of dialogue, followed by song, followed by dance, were swept away and would ever after be seen as old-fashioned. As Rodgers commented at the time, "The orchestrations sound the way the costumes look".

In other words, *Oklahoma!* changed everything. Whether Rodgers and Hammerstein intended to change the world or whether they were just writing the best musical either of them knew how to write has been argued over by theatre historians ever since. What is sure is that these two very different men – one charming, expansive and outgoing, the other dour, unsmiling, and difficult – established both a business and an artistic relationship which would last, not without some bumps, until Hammerstein's death in 1960.

Hammerstein made the decision to retain Riggs' Oklahoma vernacular in his lyrics and dialogue so that 'pretty' comes out as 'purty', 'and' is invariably 'n', and words that end in 'ing' lose their final 'g'. Instead of sounding hokey or condescending, this faithfulness to the local dialect resulted in a new theatrical language in which the actors remained true to their characters' level of education and knowledge and were therefore real. There were no stars in *Oklahoma!*, which was partly an effect of The Theatre Guild's current impoverished state, as were the simple costumes and sets. But there were many versatile actor/singer/dancers who were capable of performing the material written for them. Several of these unknowns, Alfred Drake, the original Curly, for one, and Celeste Holm, the original Ado Annie, for another, became stars as a result of their appearances in this show.

The songs, ranging from the comic 'I Cain't Say No', to the romantic 'People Will Say We're In Love', to the rousing title song (re-staged on the road by Agnes de Mille with the entire cast singing directly to the audience from the front of the stage), are not only individually tuneful and, the dialect notwithstanding, intelligent, they are collectively memorable with each song adding to the story and character until the score itself stands for the show. This is the great achievement of *Oklahoma!*, the way every element is going in the same direction, from the simple settings to Rouben Mamoulian's sensitive direction. Even the dancing.

Hiring Agnes de Mille, a choreographer with no experience of show dancing, was a real stretch. Many years later she told me how it had come about. "I had done a lot of small-scale ballets for minor companies and I had a good reputation – small but pristine – and Ballet Theatre wouldn't have given me a chance at a full-length work if it hadn't been wartime but they were stuck for a new work and so I got the job. I asked Aaron Copland for a Western-themed score and he came up with *Rodeo*. I danced the lead, The Cowgirl, on opening night and I got 19 curtain calls." By the time she told me this story she was elderly and crippled by a stroke but her eyes were shining and her tiny body vibrated with pleasure as she remembered her triumph. She leaned forward in her chair to recount the next step. "Of course, I didn't have any money. My husband was a soldier and away at the war and I had heard that the new Rodgers and Hammerstein show was going to have a Western theme too so I asked the producer, Theresa Helburn, if she'd bring them to my ballet, just in case they thought I might make their dances. I needed the money. They came backstage and asked me on the spot and that was the beginning of my Broadway career."

And what a beginning. She changed the face of Broadway dance in ways that her contemporaries couldn't have imagined. Previously, shows stopped for the dances and resumed after them. De Mille made dances that grew organically out of the action so that it was difficult to see where a dance began and ended, so integrated was it into the action. When Will Parker is describing what he has seen on his trip to Kansas City, 'Everythin's Up To Date In Kansas City', he begins to demonstrate the new dance he learned, the two-step, and this leads to a full-scale dance number which never seems incongruous because it has grown out of his fascination with the novelty of the city. Most important of all was the dream ballet that ended the first act. This long dance sequence not only embodies Laurey's dilemma in deciding between the charming Curly and the dangerous Jud, it amplifies the hopes and fears of all three characters, demonstrating their individual psychologies and laying out for the audience the various questions that will have to be answered in the second act.

What de Mille did in *Oklahoma!* affected everything that has followed it in show dance. Her influence can be seen in the work of Jerome Robbins, Michael Kidd, Bob Fosse, Michael Bennett, Gillian Lynne, and Susan Stroman as well as many contemporary ballet choreographers. Nobody dances in a musical who doesn't bear the mark of Agnes de Mille. Her work in *Oklahoma!, Carousel, Gentlemen Prefer Blondes, Paint Your Wagon* and nearly a dozen other musicals made her the pre-eminent show choreographer of the 20th century. Rodgers and Hammerstein knew talent when they saw it and knew how to use it to enhance their shows. She won every award a choreographer could win and for many years a dream ballet was *de rigeur* for every new musical.

Despite the near-bankruptcy of The Theatre Guild, or perhaps because of it, Rodgers and Hammerstein were left alone to develop this new style of musical play. Rehearsals were brisk and businesslike. If something was wrong, they didn't talk about fixing it, they fixed it. Each department reported to them, not to the nominal producers, so they knew moment by moment the progress of every element. They didn't know it at the time but they were building a machine, a business, for making musicals that would be the model for each show that followed.

Ethan Mordden's excellent book about Rodgers and Hammerstein pinpoints the exact moment when the production team knew they had something special:

> One Saturday afternoon, Mamoo decided to 'put the first act together'. That is, the actors and singers with whom *he* had been working and the dancers with whom de Mille had been working would join forces for the first time, so the production staff could see what it had…And when Laurey and the singers finished their section of 'Many a New Day'

and de Mille's corps took the stage to interpret what Laurey feels and wants but cannot directly express, stage manager Elaine Steinbeck ran to the phone, called Rodgers – Hammerstein was in the country that weekend – and said, 'You'd better get down here quick'.

Because, for the first time, the absolute dead-on rightness of Mamoulian, de Mille, and the cast, of Riggs' story and what Rodgers and Hammertsein had wrought of it, had been made palpable, visible. The story led directly to the music – made it necessary, the actors fell effortlessly into melody, and the dancers extrapolated what the melody was *about*. Suddenly the show became something very real that was just about to occur.

All through rehearsals and previews in New Haven and Boston, Rodgers and Hammerstein, de Mille, Mamoulian, and the entire production team tinkered with the show, taking out a song here, putting in a line there, changing the title from *Away We Go* to *Oklahoma*, to, very important this, *Oklahoma!*, with an exclamation mark. They couldn't seem to leave it alone until one evening after another long day of changes, Richard Rodgers said to the exhausted team, "You know what's wrong with this show? Nothing! Now everybody pipe down and let's go to bed."

And nothing was wrong with it and everything was right as the New York critics confirmed. There had been a wobbly moment when Rodgers and Hammerstein invited the producer Mike Todd to see the show out of town and he left at intermission famously proclaiming, "No gals, no gags, no chance." No way, Mr Todd.

The show ran for more than five years on Broadway and won a special Pulitzer Prize. Immediately on closing in NY there was a national tour and then another Broadway stint. In all, the original production ran for more than ten years and another three in London, breaking all possible records. *Oklahoma!* had become the gold standard, the show by which all others would be judged.

But could they do it again or was it a one-off phenomenon which would never be repeated? That one, with the benefit of hindsight, is easy to answer: there would be eight more Rodgers and Hammerstein shows, three of them certified masterpieces, one original movie musical, *State Fair,* and one television show, *Cinderella.*

Of the four great Rodgers and Hammerstein shows my favourite is *Carousel* although it's a close-run thing. Why? Perhaps because it's the darkest, the most difficult, therefore the one that carried the most risk. True, R & H were riding high on the back of the greatest success that Broadway had ever had. True, they had set up as producers of other peoples' shows, always looking for new talent and properties to manage, so they were diversified, they had written a movie musical *State Fair* which starred Will Rogers, Dick Haymes and Jeanne Crain, but, in 1944, two years after *Oklahoma!,* they had yet to start a new stage musical. And along came Theresa Helbrun again, she who had discovered *Green Grow The Lilacs,* bearing a copy of an obscure Hungarian play and insisting that it would be perfect for the next Rodgers and Hammerstein hit.

*Liliom* is a 1909 play by Ferenc Molnár about a charming ne'er-do-well who dies in the commission of a crime, set in Budapest and, er, Heaven. Why Helbrun hit on that one is a mystery but, once again, she was right. By the time R & H had finished with it, it contained some of the most sublime songs ever written for the musical theatre, but, like the Molnár play, it dealt with such serious subjects as widowhood, child abuse, theft, murder, life after death, what to do with a difficult teenager, and, above all, poverty. If *Oklahoma!* was about discovering a new future from an uncertain past, *Carousel* is about making a life worth living from the most unpromising elements. Transplanted from Hungary to New England, its characters scrape a living either from the local mills or by fishing. None is rich or sophisticated.

Enter Julie, a feisty mill girl, and Billy, a brash barker from the carnival. We know as soon as we see them together that they will fall in love and that trouble will most assuredly follow. This may be a marriage made in heaven but, if so, heaven has a very odd sense of humour. Worse, when Julie becomes pregnant, Billy is determined to make a good life for his child, even if he has to steal. He gets killed in a bungled robbery and Julie is left alone to raise their daughter, Louise. In Act Two, Louise is a rebellious teenager, just as he was, and Billy returns for one day, the day of Louise's high-school graduation, to try to help Julie and the daughter he never met. Meanwhile, Julie's best friend, Carrie, marries a local fisherman, Mr Snow, who becomes, by Act Two, a canning tycoon. Two couples, same origins, different outcomes.

*Carousel*, different though it was from *Oklahoma!*, with its own musical vocabulary and sense of destiny (as Stephen Sondheim said, "*Oklahoma!* is about a picnic, *Carousel* is about life and death"), the new show built upon what Rodgers and Hammerstein had learned in the earlier one and solidified their partnership. Now they were confidently writing scenes that ended in a song which ended in another scene. Once again they had Agnes de Mille to make dances that said in movement what their songs and dialogue could only suggest, to make manifest the emotions and feelings the characters couldn't express. And they came together with such unity of purpose that an audience avid to applaud couldn't find a gap in the action. Lyrics were themselves conversations, sometimes sung, sometimes spoken. Rodgers' music was written in *leit motifs*, like a Wagner opera, so that subliminal phrases would recur, indicating character, or place, or emotion.

The second half, after Billy's death, was problematic. Sticking closely to Molnár's play, it was clear that Hammerstein had a dilemma: he wanted to show heaven through Billy's own limited imagination but it came out as a sort of courtroom – a stern Mr God, like a magistrate, meting out justice. On the road, Boston hated it. The second act wasn't improved by Agnes de Mille's ballet which was intended to show the birth of Louise but only succeeded in slowing down the action. She reset it a dozen times on her exhausted dancers but just couldn't get it right. According to Ethan Mordden, "in one tormented moment she told Hammerstein that she hated her work and hated herself, and Hammerstein grabbed her and growled, 'Be careful, you're speaking of the woman I love.'" His joke must have done the trick because the newly reconstituted second act had a shorter ballet and a much more surreal version of heaven in which Billy meets not God but a character called The Starmaker who takes him back to earth at just the time his wife and daughter most need him.

When *Carousel* reached the Majestic Theatre on April 19th, 1945, all its on-the-road problems were behind it. Cast, like *Oklahoma!*, with unknown actors, *Carousel* made a star of John Raitt and ran for more than two years before following *Oklahoma!* into the Theatre Royal, Drury Lane in London. It had proved that a musical with a dark and serious theme could not only succeed on Broadway but triumph. It had demonstrated definitively that Rodgers and Hammerstein was not just a team but a brand, and, at the end of a long and debilitating war, it had given audiences the belief that a society of simple people with problems was worth fighting for. And if it is the least often revived of all the great Rodgers and Hammersteins, that is because it is the one that requires the most care, the best voices, and the greatest attention.

*South Pacific*, based on James Michener's rambling set of stories, was a particular labour of love for Oscar Hammerstein. Though born rich himself, he had always been interested in social issues and way back in 1927 he tackled race and inter-marriage in *Showboat*. In all his libretti, whether with Richard Rodgers or not, he usually managed to interpolate his concerns about what mattered to him, about poverty, and about ordinary Americans. He was always more interested in simple people than in the rich and well-born, telling Arnold Michaelis, "You find people who are more limited in their education, they're more likely, I think, to say what they mean."

Joshua Logan and Leland Hayward had bought the rights to Michener's book, initially to make it into a movie but they took it to Rodgers and Hammerstein who said they were interested in making a stage musical out of it but only if they controlled the production. Both had separately had their work trampled on in the past by insensitive producers and, now that they had the power to say 'no', they also had the power to say 'yes', but on their own terms. Logan wasn't happy but was somewhat mollified by being asked to direct.

*Tales of the South Pacific* told of islanders who took their living from the sea and the amazing bonus of having the US Navy based on their island, of bored sailors far from home and their girls, of planters with dodgy pasts, of military nurses and lonely young officers without enough to do, and the constant fear of the war that was going on...somewhere else.

Hammerstein carved these disparate stories into a unified whole, the story of a planter with a past who falls in love with a navy nurse from Little Rock, Arkansas. She flees from him when she discovers that he has two mixed-race children and he undertakes a dangerous mission on a neighbouring island. His partner in this wartime mission is a young officer, Lt. Cable, a carefully brought-up upper-class boy from the best part of Philadelphia. He falls desperately in love with an island girl, daughter of the local profiteer, a love story that, because of her race, has to end in disaster. Meanwhile, the Navy SeaBees, the ordinary sailors, are cooking up all kinds of schemes to allay their boredom, including a camp show, led by Nurse Nellie, in love with Emile de Becque, the planter, but seeing no future for her romance.

R & H decided that, for this one to work, they would have to reverse their previous policy and cast it with stars. At any rate, two stars. Mary Martin was the reigning queen of the Broadway stage, a musical comedy gal to her finger-tips. No delicate soprano she, but a Broadway belter who could rival Judy Garland and Ethel Merman. She was cast as

Nellie Forbush from Little Rock, who would wash her hair every night on stage and twice on Wednesdays and Saturdays, as she "washed that man right out of my hair." Opposite her, as Emile, the French planter, they cast the great Italian Metropolitan Opera star, Ezio Pinza. So terrified was Martin of having her Broadway belt compared unfavourably with his operatic baritone that Rodgers wrote the entire score without his principals having to sing together at all, save for a few lines of 'Some Enchanted Evening', usually sung on opposite sides of the stage.

Logan realised within moments of the first rehearsal that Pinza's English was almost non-existent and that his accent made him all but incomprehensible. He demanded that R & H fire him. But Pinza was a big draw and Logan was no longer a producer so they refused. By the time they opened, Pinza's Italian accent was heavy but not impenetrable and the chemistry between him and Mary Martin was sufficient to overcome any residual unease.

Throughout *South Pacific*, through the beautiful songs, the lavish staging, the funny numbers – 'There is Nothing Like a Dame', 'Honey Bun' – and the lyrical ones, the lush island settings and the intimations of war coming ever nearer, Hammerstein maintained his emphasis on the idiocy of racism. One of his songs, a masterpiece, is about how children learn to despise those of another race, 'You've Got to Be Taught', and another is about how you can't choose who you fall in love with, 'Some Enchanted Evening'. The audience loved the characters and, through them, listened to the lessons Hammerstein was teaching.

I've always loved the story of the two Dorothys – Dorothy Rodgers and Dorothy Hammerstein – at a party following the premiere of *South Pacific*. Imagine, said a man introducing his wife to Dorothy Rodgers, "Her husband wrote 'Some Enchanted Evening'." "No," interjected Dorothy Hammerstein firmly, "*my* husband wrote 'Some Enchanted Evening'. *Her* husband wrote 'la, la-la, la-la, la.'"

The origins of *The King and I* were different from any of the other R & H musicals. The British actress, Gertrude Lawrence, bored one afternoon in Los Angeles while shooting a film, took herself to see a movie called *Anna and the King of Siam*, starring Rex Harrison and Irene Dunne. In the closing credits she discovered that the film was based on a book, a true story about an Englishwoman, Anna Leonowens, and her time in Bangkok as governess to the children of the King of Siam. No stranger to the world of musicals – both George Gershwin and Noël Coward had written shows for her and she was the first British star to have her name above the title on a Broadway theatre – Gertie knew instinctively that it would make a marvellous musical and that Anna was a role she was born to play. She promptly bought the rights and took them to Rodgers and Hammerstein, begging them to make her a show.

Lawrence was stage magic – mercurial, undisciplined, funny, and endlessly talented when, that is, she wanted to bring all that to the stage. R & H were warned against her, "She's so difficult, especially when she's bored." But the meeting of these two immovable objects – Anna, a feminist fighting for her rights and The King of Siam, an absolute monarch accustomed to being obeyed, set in a totalitarian society just beginning to feel the effect of outside influences – was too good an opportunity to miss and they set about writing a show that would not bore Miss Lawrence. The result was *The King and I.*

Casting the King was easy. As Rodgers recalled in his autobiography, "He was casually dressed and carried a guitar. He scowled in our direction, sat down on the stage and crossed his legs, tailor fashion, then plunked one whacking chord on his guitar and began to howl in a strange language...He looked savage, he sounded savage and there was no denying he projected a feeling of controlled ferocity...Oscar and I looked at each other and nodded." He, of course, was Yul Brynner who had appeared in *Lute Song* but who was otherwise totally unknown.

The politics of Thailand fascinated Hammerstein, particularly how he could deal with the slavery issue without overbalancing the plot. He introduced a young woman, sent to the King as a present and her love for the high-born young man sent by the King of Burma to deliver her. The musical problems enthralled Rodgers, who wrote a long ballet score, choreographed by Jerome Robbins (as was *Shall We Dance)*, for the entertainment of visiting British diplomats, which was a Thai adaptation of *Uncle Tom's Cabin*, the anti-slavery novel by Harriet Beecher Stowe. The songs are marvellous, even more so when you accept that, by this time, Lawrence's voice, never strong, now had a tiny range which had to be accommodated by the composer.

The show opened on March 29th, 1951, to ecstatic reviews which were better for Hammerstein than for Rodgers, a source of tension between them. The show was a revelation in its innovation and depth. It needed to be, it was, at $360,000, the most expensive show in Broadway history. Brynner was an instant star and forever after was associated with that role. Lawrence was back where she belonged, in lights over Broadway. *The King and I* would continue to play for 1,246 performances on Broadway but, a year into the run, just when Gertie Lawrence was on the verge of her greatest triumph, a return to London in Coronation year starring in a hit show of her own, she fell ill. R & H asked Noël Coward, as her oldest friend, to beg her to leave the show for her own sake as well as that of their show but she wouldn't do it. She was only 54 when she died, 17 months into the run, still playing Anna, but before she had the pleasure of seeing how much the British loved her show.

Yul Brynner, though, made an entire career out of playing the King. After Lawrence's death, he played and toured with a succession of 'Annas', shifting the emphasis from her role to his, until he demanded and received sole billing for the many new productions in which he starred. Despite a queue of 'Kings' which have succeeded him, nobody has made even a dent on the indelible impression he made on audiences throughout the world. The show, the role, and the performance became one, exactly as Rodgers and Hammerstein intended.

These four musical plays, *Oklahoma!, Carousel, South Pacific,* and *The King and I,* with *The Sound of Music* following a respectable distance behind, became the cornerstone of the musical theatre in the 20th century. It is no exaggeration to point out that, had Rodgers and Hammerstein never found each other, it is impossible to imagine what the theatre today would have looked like. But they did, and so what followed owes much, if not everything, to them.

# 4. Sit Down, You're Rockin' the Boat

THE LATE KENNETH Tynan, patron saint of us theatre critics, called *Guys and Dolls* "*The Beggar's Opera* of Broadway", in a review so brilliant that it now hangs on my wall. Who am I to argue?

There are works of art which precisely reflect a sense of place – Canaletto's Venice, Greig's Norway, Marquez's Colombia, and Damon Runyon's New York. A journalist of great range – in the Teens and Twenties he covered sports, politics, social events, crime, and cinema, for the *New York American* – Runyon's apotheosis was a series of short stories about the city that was his home and which he knew better than anyone. Runyon's Broadway stories were about the low-life of Manhattan, the gamblers, petty criminals, con-men, dolls, gangsters, do-gooders, and thieves of those midtown streets "somewhere between Times Square and Columbus Circle". Women, in his parlance, were all "dolls", whether they were Salvation Army saints or Hot Box Club sinners.

Runyon's language was distinctive, a combination of present-tense street argot and high-toned, almost Shakespearean, expressionism. His characters speak formally, their New York slang blending seamlessly into a sentence structure worthy of Oscar Wilde but uniquely Damon Runyon. It is possible,

Ken Tynan's review proves it, to parody or paraphrase Damon Runyon's people but it is impossible to imagine them anywhere but New York. When he died, in 1946, his ashes were scattered along his beloved Broadway.

Runyon's stories found character in the speech patterns of his only slightly fictitious assembly. He wanted to discover the nature of the people and the town, or at least that small part of it which they inhabited, and he did it by listening to them during his long journalistic apprenticeship. Social documentary lived in people he had met in his perambulations around the racetracks, taverns, clubs and street corners of Manhattan – Harry the Horse, Sky Masterson, Nicely-Nicely Johnson, Brandy Bottle Bates, Miss Sarah Brown – all real, and he wanted them to tell their stories in their own fractured words. They just needed a little help from him. They got it in the form of the short stories he wrote for magazines such as Colliers and the *Saturday Evening Post* where all the characters who populate *Guys and Dolls* first appeared.

Frank Loesser was living in Hollywood when the suggestion of making a musical from the Broadway stories was mooted. It came from the producers, Cy Feuer and Ernest Martin, who, having produced *Here's Charley* with a score by Loesser, thought of him first when they read Runyon's stories. He started writing the songs immediately, even though he didn't yet have a libretto. Or, for that matter, a libretto writer. Or, in fact, the rights.

Feuer and Martin had chosen Jo Swerling, an experienced Hollywood hand, to write the book, under the impression that the main story they had chosen, *The Idyll of Miss Sarah Brown*, the tale of a inveterate gambler and a Salvation Army doll, would be a romantic show about mis-matched lovers like Rodgers' and Hammerstein's *South Pacific*. These were the instructions they gave Swerling who duly wrote a straightforward musical book. When Loesser saw it he knew the direction was wrong. He told the producers that what the Runyon stories needed was a crazy comedy, not a romantic plot. Loesser never cared about plots. His interests were character and situation. Plots were nice, but they shouldn't interrupt a good song. And, before the book was completed, Loesser had already written seventeen of the best songs ever written for the theatre.

The producers, convinced by Loesser that they needed a new writer, had a trawl around the literary waterfront before settling, rather surprisingly as he'd never written for the theatre before, on Abe Burrows, a well-known radio comedy writer who had gone to school in New York with producer Cy Feuer, choreographer Michael Kidd, and Loesser himself. What Burrows did was to fit the gags, the funny lines, the love stories, the gambling and the praying, Runyon himself, around the songs. This is a reversal of the usual practice of writing the book or, at least, an outline of the story first and then writing songs to fit. In his inexperience, Burrows had hit on perhaps the only method of containing the ego of the brilliant Frank Loesser – to let him lead the show with his songs instead of shoe-horning them into a pre-set formula book. Jo Swerling was furious, insisting that he had written the show and Burrows was merely "polishing". To this day he retains his writing credit although all those who were actually part of the production insist that he had nothing to do with the final version.

The uncredited genius on the book was undoubtedly the director, George S Kaufman. A play craftsman to his finger-tips, Kaufman was justly famous not only for his directing skills but for his numerous successful plays and his ability to collaborate with others. He understood exactly what a script needed and where it needed it. It was, Burrows said, like being apprenticed to a master plumber or bricklayer, realising that a play*wright* is, in fact, a man who constructs a play just as a builder constructs a building, "like a wheelwright or a ship-wright or any other kind of 'wright'", and Kaufman, he said, treated him "like a member of the bricklayers' union", someone who had to be taught where to lay the bricks of construction so that they didn't trample on the story or his own dialogue. It didn't matter how funny the joke, if the structure wasn't right, the audience wouldn't laugh. Kaufman, veteran of so many Broadway hits, knew all this instinctively and Burrows, although a highly successful comedy writer in his own right, had the good sense to know what he didn't know and to learn it from Kaufman.

I have never understood why Kaufman accepted the job of directing *Guys and Dolls* in the first place. Having loathed directing the Marx Brothers in *The Cocoanuts,* he had come to believe that plays should not be interrupted by songs. *Guys and Dolls* was certainly not his first musical, despite his dislike of them. He had directed, successfully, the Gershwins' *Strike Up the Band* and *Of Thee I Sing* which had won the first Pulitzer Prize for Drama ever given to a musical but he had no musical sense at all, was tone-deaf, and thought songs were the death of plays.

Handed Loesser's extraordinary seventeen songs for *Guys and Dolls,* he not only didn't recognise them for what they were, he actually left the theatre when Michael Kidd and the musical staff were rehearsing them. They were, he said, "lobby numbers," meaning that he could go and smoke in the lobby until the songs were over. In his autobiography, Abe Burrows contended that he overheard Kaufman complaining from the lobby, "Good God, do we have to do every number this son-of-a-bitch ever wrote?" With the competing egos of what are today known as "the creatives", particularly Loesser and Kaufman, it's a wonder *Guys and Dolls* ever got on at all.

And the songs were good. No, the songs were great. Having grown up writing funny songs, patter songs, comic situation songs, what Loesser wanted to do now was to make us cry and, if possible, make us think about good and evil. While he would go on to write a quasi-operetta, *The Most Happy Fella,* it was in *Guys and Dolls* where he struck out for entirely new territory, musically and lyrically.

Burrows and Kaufman's book, growing organically out of the songs, emphasised the none-too-hidden theme of the stories. In the pedantic 1950s good and bad, right and wrong, were dramatically limned. We had just been through a war in which Hitler was indubitably wrong and bad, Churchill and Roosevelt were equally right and good. End of contest.

But was it? What Burrows and Loesser took from Runyon was an altogether more nuanced view of life. Who was to say that a bunch of gamblers and thieves didn't have at least as strong a moral code, albeit personal, as an army of do-gooders? And what was so great about a beautiful girl, Miss Sarah Brown, denying herself love when she could have a wonderful time with a wicked gambler, Sky Masterson, in Havana? What was so bad about the gamblers who display kindness, friendship, and loyalty to each other along with a touching belief that, no matter what, everything will turn out fine? And what was so good about the rigidity of the Salvation Army rules when its members are convinced that, if they don't obey them, they're going straight to hell?

Nathan Detroit may be running "The Oldest Established Permanent Floating Crap Game In New York" and, having been chucked out of his last venue, may well be distracted whilst finding another, but his love for Miss Adelaide of the Hot Box Club is, after a fourteen-year engagement, true, and undying. It's hardly his fault that every time the word 'marriage' is mentioned she develops a psychosomatic cold.

*Guys and Dolls* is an inverted morality tale, growing out of Damon Runyon's close-up knowledge of the streets of New York, and a fable with a point – that good and evil certainly exist, but not necessarily in the places we have learned to look.

One of the oddities of the show is the way there is not one leading lady but two, not one leading man but two. The two gamblers – Sky Masterson and Nathan Detroit – are equally important. One runs the crap game, the other plays in it, and Sky only has all the best songs because, in the original cast, although Sam Levene, who played Nathan, was the perfect character actor for the part, he couldn't sing so Loesser had to cut the songs intended for him and give them to other cast members. As a result, he only has 'Sue Me', a comic song which is mostly spoken.

On the female side, Miss Sarah is the straight-laced Mission doll from the Salvation Army who falls in love with Sky against her better judgment. She has two romantic songs while Nathan's longtime fiancée, Miss Adelaide, the doll singer at the Hot Box, has at least as much stage time as Miss Sarah and it's her songs – 'Take Back Your Mink' and 'Adelaide's Lament' – that carry the girls' comic hopes and dreams. In almost every musical of the middle of the 20th century there is a second couple with a sub-plot romance in counterpoint to the leading man and lady but *Guys and Dolls* is the only one I know where both couples carry the show jointly.

For the first production the try-outs were in Philadelphia. Vivacious, blue-eyed Vivian Blaine was the first Miss Adelaide, the experienced and handsome Robert Alda (father of Alan Alda) was Sky, Isabel Bigley played Miss Sarah and Sam Levene was the definitive Nathan Detroit.

Loesser had a terrible temper and an ego to match. While in Philadephia with rehearsals that were not going well, the choreographer, Michael Kidd, wanted to try a new set of steps for a song and dance routine so he told the actors to "mark" the music so he could just concentrate on their feet. Marking is a technique where singers indicate the songlines softly to save their voices for when volume is needed. Loesser was furious. He charged to the stage and told Kidd he didn't give a damn about his dances, he wanted to hear his music and he wanted to hear it LOUD. "Loud," he proclaimed, "is good!!! All you sons of bitches work for me. Now SING!!!" Unsurprisingly, the entire cast began to bellow the song at the top of their considerable voices. Loesser backed up the aisle, pretending that he wanted to hear whether they could be heard from way back in the auditorium. He backed into the lobby and, out of sight of the cast on stage, left the theatre, cheerfully bought himself an ice-cream from a nearby stand, and walked on up the street, leaving the terrorised cast still singing.

The worst Loesser incident also occurred in Philadelphia. Isabel Bigley, a gentle girl playing Miss Sarah, had what is known as a break in her voice, a catch where the voice moves up and down the scale. Loesser was rehearsing her in 'I'll Know', one of her lovesongs, and became so incensed at the recurring problem that he leapt on to the stage and punched her in the face. She burst into tears and left the theatre and, despite flowers, chocolates, and a very expensive bracelet, she avoided him thereafter. As an amazed Loesser told his wife, apparently mystified by her wary coldness towards him, "She won't talk to me since I hit her."

The rehearsal process was messy, the dress rehearsal such a disaster that another was rapidly inserted in an already tight schedule and that was even worse. The first time they showed it to an audience, an invited group of wives, agents, friends, etc., nobody laughed at the jokes and they didn't even applaud Michael Kidd's brilliant opening number, one of the only opening numbers for any show that sets up the milieu, the street scene, and the characters but which is neither sung nor danced but resolves into a Bach-style fugue for three gamblers trying to decide which horse to bet on, 'A Fugue For Tin Horns'.

The producers panicked and demanded that Kaufman and Burrows cut the opening and the first scene. A weary cast was handed the cuts and went away to learn the new lines. The following day it became clear that the first scene had been fine all along and a by now furious cast had to unlearn what they had just been given and relearn what they had previously rehearsed. The principals were mutinous. And exhausted. "You're a bunch of amateurs," growled Kaufman to the producers as he and Burrows trudged out of the theatre to make yet more rewrites.

But they weren't. And he certainly wasn't. It was clear, opening night in Philadelphia, that they had a massive hit. Yes, there were changes to be made, cuts and additions, but it was going to be fine when they got it to Broadway. Second night, on the other hand, was a disaster. Nobody laughed, nobody applauded. But it was just an aberration, nothing serious. It was the last time *Guys and Dolls* would ever leave an audience cold. Somehow, out of the combined talents of all those artists, the cast and crew and designers who each had a job to do on a Manhattan street in Runyonland had made it work collectively and there, for all to see, was Damon Runyon and his stories in a truly great musical.

As Kenneth Tynan said, somewhere else in his Runyonesque review, "Miss Adelaide is a very choice blonde judy and she gets to sing a song which goes as follows: 'Take back your mink to from whence it came' and which hits me slap-dab in the ear as being supernaturally comical…Personally, I found myself laughing ha-ha last night more often than a guy in the critical dodge has any right to. And I am ready to up and drop on my knees before Frank Loesser."

Supernaturally comical? Of course. As usual, Tynan has it right. *Guys and Dolls* is one of the funniest shows ever written but it survives because of its supernatural ability to engage us in all of its magic.

# 5. Wouldn't It Be Loverly?

A N HOUR BEFORE the curtain was due to go up on the first perfomance of *My Fair Lady* Rex Harrison was locked in his dressing room and refusing to come out. "I'm not ready. I am *not* ready to open," he screamed from behind a locked door. Herman Levin, the producer, Moss Hart, the director, Alan Jay Lerner, the lyricist and book writer, and Fritz Loewe, the composer, all tried to persuade him. "I hate musical comedy," he yelled in rage and terror, "get Gielgud, you always wanted him anyway." Harrison, never easy, had been thrown by every small problem in rehearsal, and, never having done a musical before, the back-breaking straw was an orchestra run-through at which he wasn't able to hear the melody lines for his songs.

Despite a blizzard in New Haven, the Shubert Theatre was sold out and Harrison's agent warned him that if he didn't play he might never work again. He had started this tantrum at four in the afternoon and by 6pm the rest of the cast had been sent home and dispersed all over town. When Rex emerged at 7pm, tantrum over ("I will go on if I have to but, I warn you, I'm not ready."), Moss Hart sent his younger brother all over town to round up the cast. He stopped the movie in every cinema to yell, "Everybody from the *Fair Lady* company back to the theatre, we're opening tonight after all." He went to the local gyms and health clubs and they leapt off massage tables and exercise bikes, or left their meals half-eaten and ran to the theatre through the snow. He broadcast emergency messages on the local radio stations. By curtain time, all the actors and musicians were in their places as was Rex Harrison.

When Moss Hart called his wife that evening to tell her how it went he said, cautiously, "It's some kind of hit, I don't yet know how big." How big is the stuff of history. *My Fair Lady* may or may not be, in the words of the great critic Brooks Atkinson, "The greatest musical of the 20th century" but it is indubitably one of the most successful. It opened at the Mark Hellinger Theatre on Broadway on March 15th, 1956 and ran for 2,717 performances, nearly seven years, before an equally long run at the Theatre Royal, Drury Lane in London's West End. For all of that time, lines started at midnight for one of the 40 standing room spaces for the following day. The show won nine Tonys, the New York Drama Critics' Award (unanimously for the first time ever) and, in the first year, sold more than one million copies of the cast album. *My Fair Lady* is always in revival somewhere.

A few years ago the Old Vic mounted a fine production of George Bernard Shaw's *Pygmalion* starring Tim Pigott-Smith as Professor Henry Higgins. The only problem was, as the audience watched the play, they all simultaneously sang *My Fair Lady's* songs in their heads and, occasionally, out loud. For *Pygmalion* is a rare example of a good play which has been made into an even better musical and now, all these years later, the play seems so naked without its songs that even when they are not performed we need to add them for ourselves.

*My Fair Lady* is now so centrally part of our collective Anglo-American culture that it is almost unimaginable, albeit true, that it nearly didn't exist at all. An indefatigable Hungarian movie producer (well, he *said* he was Hungarian, actually he was Rumanian), by the name of Gabriel Pascal became obsessed with the idea that the 1914 *Pygmalion*, of which, with Shaw's own screenplay, he had already made a film, would make a great musical and offered it to every major musical maker in New York, London, and Hollywood. Everybody turned it down. Rodgers and Hammerstein had a bash at a score and then gave up, Dietz and Schwartz, Cole Porter, and even Noël Coward toyed with it for a while before deciding that the play was fine as it was and didn't need to be a musical at all. Hammerstein, never one to shirk the unconventional, said, after a year of trying, that he and Dick Rodgers couldn't find a way to turn Shaw into a show with a conventional love story and a happy ending.

Poor Mr. Pascal died before Frederick Loewe and his erudite partner, Alan Jay Lerner, took it on, which they did while the rights were still in dispute between Pascal's ex-wife and his mistress. Instead of trying to make a musical by simplifying the story and the characters in the usual way of adaptations and jettisoning the rest for showbiz purposes, they decided to

incorporate their songs into Shaw's play. Rather than cannibal-
ise it and leave it for dead, their concept was to keep as much of
the play as possible and to use as much of Shaw's language and
imagery as could be crammed into the book and lyrics.

What the highly intelligent Lerner had understood was that
Shaw's play was, under all the delicious jokes, about a serious
subject, one of real importance in the prosperous '50s when
soldiers who had returned from the Second World War were
wanting a different, more equal life than they had left. Lerner
knew that *Pygmalion* was actually about social status, women's
rights, and the possibility of moving across class barriers to a
better life. If Henry Higgins can make a flower seller from the
streets of Covent Garden into a lady, then anyone can change
their life for the better. In 1954, when he started writing, this
was an immediate and pressing concern as it had been for GBS
himself.

Once that decision was made, they kept the 1914 setting
because it would allow them to recreate the social condi-
tions of London (and, by extension, other cities of the world),
demonstrate the enormous gap between the upper classes and
the working poor, and the abject position of poor women in
particular as chattels and worse, which was a perennial interest of Shaw.

Now, more than 50 years later, *My Fair Lady* seems to us the
epitome of a classic musical with its period setting, its traditional melodic structure, its clever Shavian lyrics, and its beau-

tiful sets and costumes. But don't be fooled; this is a radical show, one which broke all the rules technically and textually and which had as much chance of failing disastrously as succeeding triumphantly.

Until this show, musicals were all constructed around a love story, one that could only end in marriage or death. *My Fair Lady*'s central characters are a young girl, a middle-aged professor of phonetics, an elderly English colonel, a grand old woman, and a disreputable London dustman. Not much opportunity for romance there. Freddie Eynsford-Hill, who falls in love with Eliza, is a minor irritation, important because he sings the show's only lovesong, 'On The Street Where You Live'. Until *My Fair Lady* there had always been two plots – a main story and a sub-plot involving other unrelated characters. As in Shaw, here there was only one – the makeover of a street urchin into a young woman who could pass herself off as belonging to a higher class and therefore able to make a better life for herself. All the rich incidents in the book, the film, and the play are bent towards the same end.

Musicals had always had a chorus, multiple extras whose presence signified mood and locale. While Lerner and Loewe introduced two rousing numbers for Eliza's dustman father ('Get Me To The Church On Time' and 'With A Little Bit Of Luck') incorporating his friends in the pub, a ball where Eliza fools another phoneticist that she is a Hungarian princess, and a spectacular scene at Ascot, including the entire cast, these are exceptions. In fact, almost all of *My Fair Lady* is constructed of intimate scenes devoted to Eliza's transformation.

Most importantly, dramatic realism and serious themes in musicals were to be avoided at all costs, lest the audience not be entertained. Here we have issues of poverty and class, political and social injustice, and the struggle for personal freedom for a girl who, even in the 1950s, would have been considered lucky just to become a maid in Higgins' household in Wimpole Street.

Lerner chose to work mostly from Shaw's own screenplay for the film of *Pygmalion,* knowing that GBS had been satisfied with the movie and thought Wendy Hiller's Eliza close to perfect. Aware that Shaw had been violently opposed to musicalisation of his work ever since he saw *The Chocolate Soldier*, Oscar Strauss' operetta of *Arms and the Man*, which he hated, Lerner realised that Shaw had, with the film, solved some of the staging problems of *Pygmalion* and borrowed liberally from them for the musical.

*Pygmalion* is itself an adaptation, although very free, of a Greek myth in which a misogynistic sculptor falls in love with his own creation, a statue called Galatea, prays to Apollo to bring his ivory goddess to life and, when he does, marries her. Shaw was interested both in Pygmalion's hatred of women and in what would happen to a girl who was the creation of a master. Lerner further developed both these themes in *My Fair Lady* with Higgins' exasperated 'Why Can't a Woman be More

Like a Man?' and with Eliza's vindictive 'Without You' and 'Just You Wait'. The ongoing dislike and mistrust of women is equally demonstrated by Prof. Higgins and Col. Pickering's refusal to see Eliza as anything but the engine of their experiment, and Doolittle's avowed belief, expressed in dialogue and in both his big numbers, that women exist to serve men but that men must always be wary of being 'caught' by them.

It would be disingenuous not to acknowledge that the instantaneous success of *My Fair Lady* owed much to the subtlety of its director, Moss Hart, and, above all, to the casting of Rex Harrison as Higgins. Hart, himself a gifted writer, worked from the inception with Lerner and Loewe as the show took shape and it is impossible to over-estimate his contribution, not least his brave decision to engage Rex Harrison who was well known to be 'difficult' and who had never done a musical before. It is true that John Gielgud was at first considered and although Noël Coward would have been wonderful, he was known to hate appearing in other people's work so the suggestion was clearly a non-starter.

In rehearsal, Harrison fought Hart every inch of the way, insisted on having his own way, terrorised poor Julie Andrews and insulted the distinguished conductor Franz Allers. He had regular screaming tantrums where he demanded that this stagehand or that chorus singer be fired for some real or imagined slight and made outrageous demands on rehearsal time, frequently co-opting a whole afternoon's rehearsal for just one of his songs.

One day, when Harrison was having difficulty with a particular line, he asked where Lerner had found it. "I wrote it," Lerner said. From there on, Harrison asked about every line he didn't like and, unless he could be reassured that Shaw had written it, would refuse to say it. But Lerner soon got wise and, if it were not from *Pygmalion*, would announce that he had taken it from one of GBS's obscure letters or essays or reviews. Harrison even bought a Penguin copy of the Shaw text and would scour it for Lerner mistakes. "Where's my Penguin," he would roar, and then hold up the rehearsal while he found the offending line. Eventually, Lerner bought a stuffed penguin from a taxidermist and the next time Rex yelled, "Where's my Penguin," the stuffed bird was wheeled out on stage to gales of laughter from the company.

But, impossible though he was, those of us who saw him witnessed one of the great performances of the age. As written, Henry Higgins is, like Rex himself, a thoroughly unlikeable man, an egotist with no thought for any but himself, a selfish academic with no human feelings, a son whose only close relationship is with his mother, a thoughtless boss, an unreliable friend, a snob, and a man who not only hates women but most of the rest of humanity as well. As played by Rex Harrison, Higgins had warmth, insight, elegance, and a touching vulnerability. He could touch a nerve in the audience which allowed them to laugh at his frailties and still pull for his success. He could make us understand how important his work was to him no matter how risible it might have been to us and he could charm us into believing that he was simply misunderstood, not uncaring.

He looked marvellous – tall, slim, wearing Cecil Beaton's clothes with the kind of insouciance that made every man in the audience envy him and every woman want to be seen with him – and, although he didn't actually sing (instead using rhythmic speaking on key, what the Germans call *sprech-stimme*) he spoke his songs with the verve and care that made them as meaningful as spoken dialogue. He was rude to every-one and the cast and crew soon learned to avoid him when offstage but onstage his acting was dazzling enough to make up for all his shortcomings (Julie Andrews once threw his slip-pers in rehearsal and they slipped from her hand and hit him full in the face; the entire company applauded) but what the audience saw was a great actor at the top of his game. What the audience saw was Henry Higgins to the life.

Julie Andrews was a different story. The first choice for Eliza was, inevitably, the queen of Broadway musicals, Mary Martin, who had got wind of the show and asked to meet the writing team. Lerner thought privately that she was too old and too American to play a young Cockney girl but, as he later wrote, "one never knows the limits of a great star's talent" and it isn't every day that a surefire star is interested in being in your show. With considerable confidence, Lerner and Loewe went to her apartment and played for her five of the classic *My Fair Lady* songs that have now been part of our collective hearts for fifty years. She hated them. "Oh, those dear boys," she moaned to her husband, "how could it have happened? They've lost all their talent." So, somewhat to Lerner's relief, Mary Martin was out.

Moss Hart had heard of a young girl, only 19 years old, who had come from England to star in a small British musical, Sandy Wilson's *The Boyfriend*. She was pretty, charming, with a crystal clear soprano and, having been a child star, not without experience. Lerner went to see the show and was instantly sold, "From the moment she set foot on the stage, one could see she fairly radiated with some indefinable substance that is the difference between talent and star." Best of all, she was young and English.

Predictably, Rex Harrison took against her, especially when she habitually practiced scales at the top of her voice and apparently in his face. After the first five days of rehearsal he stormed out proclaiming, "If this bitch is here on Monday, I'm leaving the show." And the indisputable fact was, she wasn't very good. In fact, Hart, who didn't meet her until the first rehearsal, said she wasn't getting any better and she didn't have a clue what her part really entailed. It's one thing to be a nice middle-class polite English girl playing a nice middle-class polite English girl in *The Boyfriend* and quite another to play a ragamuffin Cockney who is carrying a big Broadway musical. Not surprisingly, she was nervous.

After the first week Hart knew something drastic had to be done. He dismissed the company and holed up with Julie for two days in the New Amsterdam Theatre on 42nd St, just the two of them and a single assistant. For seven hours a day he force-fed Eliza to her, how she moved, how she felt, how she sounded. Julie said later, "He made me infuriated and scared and mad and frightened and in awe and full of an inferiority complex. He worked and worked on me…I didn't know what Eliza should be. Moss supplied the route and as the nights went by I absorbed Eliza more and more."

When they returned to rehearsals after the mini-break, other members of the cast were amazed by the transformation she had made. Miles Kreuger, now a distinguished expert on the musical theatre, was the assistant who had been present throughout the 'boot-camp', "…she had it all in there, way down deep somewhere, because it was like lifting the veils. And two days later, when rehearsals resumed, Julie Andrews was, full-blown, the Julie Andrews we know today."

Even so, she was always better in the later scenes than as the Cockney flower girl. Even today, on the original cast recording, made on the Sunday following their triumphant Broadway opening, you can still hear the cut-glass English theatre voice peeking out through her Cockney on 'Wouldn't

It Be Loverly?', like an upper-class schoolgirl with a grubby face slumming it in Covent Garden.

*My Fair Lady,* both in conception and in production, had several other elements that contributed to its success, from Stanley Holloway's unforgettable Doolittle where he somehow managed to combine cheeky élan with real menace, to Oliver Smith's painterly sets, to the irascible Cecil Beaton's stylish costumes. What strikes me now, looking back over many years since I saw the original trio at Drury Lane, is not that they were all so good but that nothing, absolutely nothing was wrong. There was no jarring moment or element, not one.

It was *My Fair Lady* that made me a musicals addict. I was 10 years old when it opened on Broadway and my only rich auntie brought me the original cast album back from New York. I still have it. By the time I was 11 years old I could sing every song in the original cadences and accents, complete with the accompaniment. I wore that first LP so thin that it looks like lace, almost transparent. It won't play any more but I'll never give it away despite having at least two CDs with the same cast, because it was playing it over and over again that made me aware of the quality of this show. There isn't a single song on this album that doesn't stand alone and, conversely, every song drives the show forward so that, taken collectively, the songs *are* the show. So many of the lyrics are taken directly from Shaw that you don't even miss the playwright, even without the dialogue. On the other hand, the play without the songs, however well played and directed, lacks something which has become vital.

Often overlooked is that Frederick Loewe's music does something different from every musical that came before. Listen to the melodies; unlike contemporary shows where the music is at odds with the subject matter, *My Fair Lady*'s is all of a piece with its period. In 1914 skirts were getting shorter, Victorian long dresses were (slowly) giving way to Edwardian silhouettes and making it easier for women to dance. What does this mean for the music? It takes notice of the turn of the century musical structure and of the way people actually moved in 1914, the year in which it is set, so it sounds as though it might have been written at that time. But Loewe has written music that is entirely contemporary for his 1950s time. The orchestration uses instrumentation that would not have been available in 1914 and there are dissonances that would have been unheard of then. Lerner wrote admiringly of his writing partner that he could "musically characterise period or a locale without losing his individuality and, at the same time, make it contemporary." And that, of course, is exactly what is needed for a modern musical set in a previous era.

Although they wrote other successful musicals – *Brigadoon, Paint Your Wagon, Camelot* – it is this one where the lyrics so perfectly match the music, syllable by syllable and note for note as though they were written by one man (Cole Porter once stared in mock amazement at Richard Rodgers and Oscar

Hammerstein and demanded, "You mean it takes *two* of you to write a musical?").

In the case of *My Fair Lady*, though, two are better than one. Because they made a masterpiece. Like the other perfect musicals in this book, *My Fair Lady* changed the face of the contemporary theatre and, together, Shaw, Lerner, Loewe, Hart and their colleagues made something that will last longer than my precious 50-year-old LP recording of the original cast. They made a show that displays all that is best about the theatre and more because it illuminates serious subjects without talking down to the audience. It gives George Bernard Shaw another avenue of communication without diminishing his genius. And it continues to entertain audiences everywhere.

And why does it all matter? Because masterpieces always matter.

# 6. Something's Coming

WHEN I MOVED to New York in 1978 I told the real estate agent that I wanted to live on the West Side of Manhattan, "somewhere within walking distance of Carnegie Hall on West 57th Street (where I would be working), and also within walking distance of Zabar's (the great delicatessen on 81st and Broadway)." I was joking about Zabar's. To my delight, she found me a 26th floor apartment overlooking Central Park and the Hudson River, nine minutes walk from Carnegie and 13 minutes from Zabar's. As we entered the building, she gestured at the magnificent newly constructed buildings of Lincoln Center, home of the Metropolitan Opera, the New York Philharmonic, NYC Ballet, NYC Opera, and the two theatres which make up the premiere arts complex of the USA and said, casually, "Of course you know, that's where *West Side Story* was set."

I was thrilled. Whatever might have been wrong with that flat I had to have it. I paid the first month's rent on the spot and I live there still. This part of Manhattan's West Side no longer looks like the mean streets where the Jets and the Sharks fought it out but even when I moved in, more than 30 years ago, neither was it a maze of tenements inhabited by dangerous gangs but a city neighbourhood with more musicians, actors, and dancers per square foot than 'civilians' with regular jobs. In the lifts in my building, you saw far more instrument cases than briefcases and the cacophony of many musical instruments practising was the predominant afternoon sound in the hallways. I loved it then, love it now, as the real-life show business world lives all around me. It is not so much that *West Side Story* is happening but that those who made it – Jerome Robbins, Stephen Sondheim, Leonard Bernstein, Arthur Laurents – echo down the years in the same geographical space together with their present-day counterparts. And it all started here. Where I live.

Or, rather, it started around 1593 on another continent where William Shakespeare imagined a love story set in the beautiful medieval town of Verona, a town which, so far as we know, he never visited. The two protagonists, he decided, would belong to clans who were at war with one another and their love would therefore be doomed. It would have to end, he concluded, in death. He called it *Romeo and Juliet*.

A mere 346 years later, in 1949, director/choreographer Jerome Robbins was asked by his friend and sometime lover, the actor, Montgomery Clift, how he could bring the somewhat passive role of Romeo to life and it set him thinking about "how to transpose this violence of emotion to the world today." According to theatre historian Keith Garebian, Robbins was "struck by the intensity of adolescent feeling" in *Romeo and Juliet*. Were there still feuds so deadly that they could lead to murder? Could it happen in, say, New York City? And, if it could, what kind of people or events were likely to generate such institutional hatred? At first, he was thinking in terms of Jews and Catholics on the Lower East Side but that conflict, while subject to occasional flare-ups, had long since settled into uneasy truces between neighbours.

No, a more likely territorial battle was still raging between two sets of Catholics – the established Polish immigrants and their Puerto Rican counterparts who, newly arrived in New York, wanted the same neighbourhoods, the same square footage, the same blocks and tenements, and were willing to fight for them. The young, poor and disenfranchised by their lack of education and jobs, formed themselves into gangs, huddled together for protection, and fought for territory as a means of establishing their right to be in this frightening new place. Jews or Puerto Ricans, what Robbins saw was a sub-culture of restless young people desperate, in spite of their differences, to be Americans. What, he asked himself, if a Jewish girl fell in love with a Catholic boy? About the same, he reasoned, as happened when a Montague fell in love with a Capulet.

He took his idea to Arthur Laurents, already an established playwright, and then to the composer Leonard Bernstein. In his diary that night Bernstein wrote, "Jerry R. called today with a noble idea: a modern version of *Romeo and Juliet* set in the slums…making a musical that tells a tragic story in musical comedy terms…can it succeed? It never has in our country." Bernstein was enthusiastic but had a full schedule – composing, conducting, and playing, all over the world. He wanted to write the music and the lyrics but couldn't see when he would find the time. Convinced that he was the only composer for the project, Robbins and Laurents opted to wait for a gap in his diary. In the event, they waited eight years.

But, although the project changed radically in that time, from the Lower East Side to the West Side and from Jews to Puerto Ricans, the three original collaborators never lost their enthusiasm from their first get-together in June 1949, "I remember that evening in Jerry's apartment as though it were yesterday," Bernstein said, later, "because of the excitement." At that meeting, Laurents wrote, they talked of the balcony scene "on a gossamer fire escape; the language lifted above modern street level until it soared into song at the moment the lovers first kissed. At that moment the surrounding buildings would disappear, leaving the lovers in space, in their own world." Their friend Nora Kaye, the ballerina, knowing all three personalities and egos, scoffed at the vision of the three of them ever working together, "You'll never write it. Your three temperaments in one room? The walls will come down."

But write it they did. While they were waiting for Bernstein to free himself to compose the music, Laurents started writing the scenario, based on *Romeo and Juliet*, and Robbins immersed himself in New York's gang culture. He watched how young people spoke, how they dealt with adults and authority figures, above all, how they moved. An idea was beginning to emerge that what had been tentatively titled *East Side Story* and then *Gangway!* should express itself in dance, that teenagers, naturally inarticulate even without the additional barriers of language, would be more inclined to dance their loves and their angers, their frustrations and gratifications, than to speak them.

Eventually, in 1955, with *Wonderful Town* and *Candide* under his belt, Bernstein returned to 'the *Romeo* project'. "All I can say is that there are moments which are right for certain things and that moment seemed to have come." Once he was dealing with Puerto Ricans instead of Jews, it all took shape for him. "Suddenly it all springs to life," he wrote in his diary, "I hear rhythms and pulses – and, most of all, I can sort of feel the form." It was madness for Bernstein to take on the lyrics as well as the music and so, when one evening Arthur Laurents met the young Stephen Sondheim at a party, he asked him whether he would like to write the words to Bernstein's music. As soon as Bernstein heard the young composer's lyrics for *Saturday Night* he offered him the job. To his surprise, Sondheim didn't jump at the chance to work with these three much more famous artists. He wanted to write his own musicals, words *and* music and he feared that what became *West Side Story* would interrupt his plans. Oscar Hammerstein, his mentor and surrogate father, tried to persuade him this was too good an opportunity to miss. Sondheim remained unconvinced, "But," he wailed, "I've never been poor and I've never even *met* a Puerto Rican." But eventually he allowed Hammerstein to persuade him that working with these three established professionals could do him nothing but good. Sondheim was on board.

The next hurdle was a serious one and nearly derailed the entire project. No Broadway producer wanted to be involved with *West Side Story*. What? A musical about street urchins with two corpses centre stage at the end of the first half and the hero dead in a shoot-out at the final curtain? "I don't know how many people begged me to stop wasting my time on something that couldn't possibly succeed," Bernstein wrote later.

The brave Roger Stevens said yes but he wouldn't take it on alone. Cheryl Crawford of the Theatre Guild agreed to join him but then got cold feet. She called a meeting in her office and told Bernstein, Robbins, Laurents and Sondheim that it was all too depressing and, unless they rewrote the entire show, she was withdrawing. Shocked but resolute, the quartet stood up and walked out in silence. They called Roger Stevens collect from a payphone and he steadied the ship. "Keep working," he said, "we'll find the money somehow." They held several backers' auditions which raised not a single cent. The subject matter and the completely new way they wanted to handle it were just too much for the conservative money men. Then Sondheim, the youngest and newest of the team, brought in a friend, Harold Prince and his partner Robert Griffith, to listen to a Sunday morning run-through. They said that if the creatives would wait until they had opened another show they'd consider raising the money and producing it.

Two months later the financing was in place and they had booked their Broadway opening for September 26th 1957, preceded by five weeks of tryouts in Washington and Philadelphia. Robbins had a tantrum just before rehearsals began and announced that he couldn't both choreograph and direct. Prince called his bluff by insisting that, if Robbins withdrew, so would the producers, and, from then on, Robbins was in complete creative charge of what was to be included in the final show. Laurents and even Bernstein deferred to him and the language of the show was then dominated by movement. He took nearly a year to find dancers who didn't look like dancers, ordinary-looking street kids for the gang members, none of whom had ever been in a Broadway show before. They all had to be able to sing and act as well as dance. Above all, no stars.

For the principals, he had to choose between singers who could dance – Anna Maria Alberghetti and Frank Poretta – and dancers who could sing – Carol Lawrence and Larry Kert. It is hardly surprising, given his ballet background, that he went with the trained dancers. The audition process was exhaustive and exhausting. Carol Lawrence was called back nine times. Kert didn't even try for the lead initially because, he said, Robbins had announced that he was looking for a tall blond Polish tenor for Tony whereas Kert was average height, dark, and Jewish. They auditioned together and apart, in the light, in the dark and, on one occasion, at the top of a rickety ladder until, eventually, they were the chosen pair.

But getting the parts was just the beginning. Robbins, accustomed to working with ballet dancers who are trained to do whatever the choreographer tells them, treated his cast as serfs. He screamed, he insulted, he belittled, he *never* praised. Said Larry Kert, "His tolerance level is too low so, if you don't give him what he wants, in a way, he destroys you." Carol Lawrence went further, saying, "The fact that one can never attain perfection did not deter him for a second. That was what he wanted and if he ended up killing you in the interim, well, that was okay too. And he was brutal, he would humiliate us, always in front of the entire company." Interestingly, both Kert and Lawrence added that they would work for him again in a heartbeat. Like Bernstein, they regarded him as a flawed genius but a genius nonetheless, "Nobody working with, or contemplating working with Jerry doesn't know to expect wounds. It goes with that particular, very talented territory," said Bernstein, who had already worked with him on *Wonderful Town, On The Town,* and the ballet *Fancy Free* before embarking on *West Side Story*.

During rehearsals, Robbins dressed the actors in the rival gangs in jackets saying 'Sharks' or 'Jets' and incited real animosity between them even offstage. He wouldn't allow them to eat lunch together and would even tell them that the other gang was plotting against them to encourage them to dislike one another. They addressed one another by their characters' names and invented complete back stories for themselves. The loneliest member of the cast was always Lee Becker, who played Anybodys, a girl dressed as a boy who wanted to be a member of the gang but was rejected by them. She ate lunch on her own every day. There was not a day when one or several members of the cast didn't leave the rehearsal room in tears, having been savaged by Robbins. Craig Zadan, producer and author, wrote, "I think that all the people who worked with him became the equivalent of abused children."

Laurents' book is short and tight. Nothing is wasted. Whatever can be done in music, in lyrics, in dance, is not said in dialogue. During the writing and rehearsal period, it was often Laurents who would suggest that a scene he had worked on for weeks might work better in another form. His introduction of Tony, a beautifully written description intended to be spoken early in the show, was scrapped to become Sondheim's lyric for Tony's first song 'Something's Coming'. He would say, "Can you do that musically?" or, "That could be a dance," always sacrificing his words for the best way. But he did invent a new language, a stylised way of speaking that, although not the way kids actually talked, did differentiate between the gangs. A child when *West Side Story* opened in London, I remember using his made-up words in conscious imitation of Jettalk. It was that specific. Bernstein's music, on the other hand, was written in many styles – Mambo, cool and jazzy, romantic and humorous, contemporary and operatic, even vaudevillian, whatever suited the dramatic moment. It was only years later, listening to the orchestral suite, that I realised how unified and related was his musical vocabulary for this show.

*West Side Story* is not a perfect match for *Romeo and Juliet*. There are adult characters in the musical but the maturity of the Duke, the elder Capulets and Montagues, and the Priest, has no equivalent in Officer Krupke or Doc. No grown-ups ameliorate the hostility of the youth here. Nobody sounds a word of warning that the kids might heed. The adults don't carry the same significance as the teenagers who make up the gang members and their girls.

Robbins had to find a way to start the show which would indicate who all the gang members are, why they hate the rival gang, what they are hostile about. Arthur Laurents spent a month writing a scene in Doc's candystore to tick all the introductory boxes. Then he threw it out because Robbins' totally innovative way of handling the introduction, to the show and to the characters, was a long Prologue in dance. This had never been done before and it set the mood for the entire evening. During the Prologue we learn who is who. And what. Bernstein's music and Robbins' choreography grows in menace throughout the scene until the hostility between the gangs erupts into violence only narrowly avoided by the arrival of the police, heralded by a police whistle. We know that this is unfinished business; the gangs are spoiling for a rumble. There is, already, an undercurrent of tragedy. The Prologue has told us that we are at the beginning of something remarkable and we unconsciously lean forward in our seats. What will happen next?

Reviews for the Broadway opening were mixed. It was a hit but not a smash. Slowly, though, audiences found it. It played for more than 700 performances at Broadway's Winter Garden Theatre, went on tour, and then returned to Broadway for 250 more. The quartet – Bernstein, Robbins, Laurents, and Sondheim – had between them produced one of the transcendent Broadway musicals of all time. Four years later, the not-very-good (except for the dance sequences) movie won ten Oscars including one for Robbins who had, in fact, been fired for being unable to stick to a budget or a shooting schedule.

Laurents and Robbins fell out before the show opened in New York and not just because Robbins had "named names" in front of the House Un-American Activities Commitee. Robbins had insisted on a credit which reads "Conceived, Choreographed, and Directed by Jerome Robbins." Worse, he had appended to Laurents' "Book by Arthur Laurents" a line which read "Based on a conception by Jerome Robbins." When Laurents pointed out that this was not true because, although Robbins had come up with the urban *Romeo and Juliet* concept, it was Bernstein and Laurents himself who had imagined the Puerto Rican/Polish American setting which was the basis for the Book. Robbins agreed but refused to remove it, "You're right, but it's too important to me," was his only defence for hogging the 'Conceived' credit that rightly belonged to three of the four original collaborators.

*West Side Story* is about alienation and belonging – to a country, to a culture, to a society, to a family, to another person. It is about every irrational conflict that is irreconcilable because it is based on faith or fear. It is always fresh because feuds are, unfortunately, all around us. The truth of *West Side Story* presents itself in the rival street gangs of the 1950s, in the Tutsis and the Hutus of Rwanda, the Catholics and Protestants in Northern Ireland, the Israelis and the Arabs in the Middle East, and in the fictionalised and Anglicised Italy of Shakespeare's 16th century. Wherever people feel they must fight rather than talk, they will have differences that cannot be reconciled.

In the final moments of *Romeo and Juliet* the Montagues and the Capulets join hands over the bodies of their dead children, finally understanding that they must heal their feud because it has caused the loss of what they held most dear. But the ending of *West Side Story*, while a certifiable tear-jerker, is less defin-itive because the touching procession where the Sharks and the Jets together carry away Tony's corpse suggests a tempo-rary and somewhat contrived truce. Tomorrow, the audience senses, there will be another rumble and more of these disenfranchised and disgruntled young men will die. Just as today's conflicts will continue on and more young men will fight and die for reasons they themselves don't understand. This is why we cry for them and why *West Side Story* is so alive, more than sixty years on.

# 7. Let Me Entertain You

W HAT IS THE American dream? It's the belief, no, the *determination* that your children will have a better life than you. *Gypsy* is the 1959 musical where a combination of Arthur Laurents' book, Jule Styne's music, Stephen Sondheim's lyrics, and Jerome Robbins' direction, broke the mould of the conventional musical and changed the face of American musical theatre. In so doing, they demonstrated once again the power and the mythology of the American dream.

The undisputed queen of burlesque in the 1930s and 1940s was the stripper Gypsy Rose Lee. Elegant, ladylike, she paraded around the stage in beautiful clothes, slowly paring them away to discreet but sexy underwear, suggesting, and yet never showing, her naked body, always keeping some part of herself hidden, no matter how much she revealed. Gypsy Rose Lee was alluring, mysterious, sexually inviting, and unique, a stripper who was a million miles from today's pole-dancers and lap-dancers. Men wanted her and women envied her, even while they made catty remarks about her to each other. Thrice married and divorced, her lovers numbered some of the most successful and famous men of her time. She special-ised in producers, had a long affair with the film director Otto Preminger by whom she had a son, and shorter ones with the likes of the showmen Billy Rose and Mike Todd. Her clothes were made by Dior and Balenciaga and she rode around in a maroon and grey Rolls Royce with her initials in gold on the door.

But by February 1956 she was approaching 45 and, realising that she couldn't expect to continue taking off her clothes in public for much longer without becoming a joke, she decided to reinvent herself. Locking herself and her 12-year-old son in a cheap motel, she embarked on the writing of a remarkable autobiography with, wrote her son in his own autobiography *Gypsy and Me,* "the kind of obsessive intensity that marked everything she did." Her compulsive writing paid off. The book is wildly entertaining, full of incident and anecdotes, in which, among other things, she reveals that she had once been Louise Hovick, the unloved elder daughter of the stage mother to end all stage mothers.

Rose was not only the mother from hell – selfish, thoughtless, careless, a liar, a cheat, a thief, a bully – she was the embodiment of the American dreamer gone rogue. She was like a steam-roller, sweeping away anything that might be in the path to what she wanted and what she wanted was stardom for her younger daughter, June, later June Havoc, the movie actress. She pushed and pushed and pushed, inventing 'acts' for June, dragging her and her sister all over the country, through every sleazy vaudeville circuit, from town to town. She all but kidnapped other kids to work in the act, abandoned them on the road, slipped out of their crummy hotels without paying, did whatever she had to do to ensure that "Baby" June got noticed. Louise was back-up, a clumsy second-best until the teenage June finally rebelled and ran away with a dancer in her act.

Anyone else would have given up and gone home to Seattle at that point but not Rose. She just took a deep breath and a belated good look at Louise, decided she wasn't as hopeless as she had always thought, and continued on her remorseless pursuit of stardom, this time with a new focus. Louise, though, couldn't sing and dance as well as June so when the star stripper of the sleazy girly burlesque where they were booked disappeared, it was Rose who said, "My daughter can do that." As she writes in her memoir, Louise, who had, by now, grown into a stunningly beautiful girl, was terrified but Rose, as always, rode roughshod over her embarrassment and stagefright, "Just parade about a bit in your slip and then drop a shoulder-strap," she bellowed at her daughter who was almost paralysed with fear.

The rest, as they say, is history. Finding her true vocation as a high-class stripper, Louise first reverted to the name on her birth certificate, Rose Louise, dropping Hovick. Soon, though, she dropped Louise in favour of Lee, thus completing her transformation into Gypsy Rose Lee. Over the years she gave a number of origins for the name Gypsy but the most obvious is that she added it on a whim and it stuck. There are other possibilities. Gypsies are a travelling people, they have no permanent home and one of her explanations was that she saw herself as a homeless entertainer forever on the road. The term 'gypsy' also refers to show dancers, usually chorus dancers who move from show to show, faceless and nameless, always working but without becoming stars. This too was what she had been for so many years travelling around as part of her sister's 'boys' chorus, never being seen in her own right.

She began to talk and sing as she paraded around the stage, taking her clothes off, becoming as well-known for her witty, self-deprecating verses and lyrics as for her perfect body. As her fortunes rose, as she played better and better theatres, she had less and less need for Rose who resented deeply her daughter's independence and lost no opportunity to remind her of exactly who had put her at the top of her profession. Theatre historian Keith Garebian writes that Rose, on her deathbed in 1954, warned both her daughters, "Wherever you go, as long as either of you lives, I'll be right there – and I swear before God you're always going to know it. You'll know I'm there, I'll see to that."

Gypsy's autobiography was a publishing sensation and nobody, including Gypsy, ever claimed that it was literally true or that the stories in it had not been highly coloured and, in some cases, invented out of whole cloth. She had learned the lessons her mother taught – that if you're going to tell a whopper, it had better be a big whopper and that nobody cared if it wasn't true so long as it was fun, sexy, and entertaining.

David Merrick wasn't the only theatrical producer who was interested in adapting it for the stage. She said subsequently that she sold him the rights for only $4000 because he reminded her of the young Mike Todd with whom she had been in love and in whom she had invested at the height of her fame. What she didn't know at the time was that Merrick hadn't even read the book. He had read a chapter in a magazine and solely on the basis of that he had entered the bidding war for the rights. Warner Brothers had, in fact, offered her $200,000 for the screen rights but, as usual, her unerring business instinct and drive, inherited from her mother, made her think that the stage adaptation might, in the long run, net her more. After all, she reassured her incredulous son, "if the show is successful I'll get royalties from it for the rest of my life as well as at least that much when it's sold for a film." When it was explained to her that the focus of the musical would not be on her but on her mother, she said that her only stipulation was that it be called *Gypsy* no matter what it turned out to be about.

Initially, Merrick recruited Jule Styne to write the music and Styne's old friends and collaborators, Betty Comden and Adolph Green, to write the book and lyrics. But the three of them just couldn't find the key to the characters and eventually returned their advance. The project sat around for a while until Merrick's co-producer, the agent Leland Hayward, had a brilliant idea. He asked Jerome Robbins to direct the show and he, in turn, said he would consider it only if Arthur Laurents would write the book. Laurents was still raw about Robbins' insistence on credits he wasn't entitled to during *West Side Story* but, having read the book and been told, not about Gypsy herself but about her sexy blonde mother ("Very sweet and an absolute killer"), he knew that *Gypsy* had the potential to be a ground-breaking show, "I wasn't going to allow personal problems to get in the way of a good project."

Personal problems were also at the root of June Havoc's surprise refusal to sign the release which would allow them to adapt her sister's book. It was one thing to allow Louise to foist an alternative reality of their joint childhood on the reading public, quite another to allow her fabrications of their early life to be reshaped by a team of writers outside the family. Laurents went ahead anyway but with no guarantee that June would allow the story of the book to be translated into a stage play. She proved so intransigent that, eventually, Merrick ordered Laurents to write June out of the story altogether, inventing a new character called Baby Claire. Only then, when it seemed she was going to be 'disappeared' from her own life, did June Havoc agree to the production.

Laurents realised that the focus and leading character of *Gypsy* had to be Rose, "a mother who lives her childrens' lives" and ends up by destroying herself. Consequently, it was

Laurents who knew that the most important next step had to be the casting of a star actress to play Rose. The unanimous choice was Ethel Merman but before he had a chance to approach her, according to Keith Garebian, she herself went to a party at Gypsy Rose Lee's New York townhouse and in her customary, self-effacing manner, accosted her, "I've read your book. I love it. I want to do it. I'm going to do it. And I'll shoot anyone else who gets the part."

Merman, Broadway's leading lady, had many talents which mainly rested in her extraordinary voice and her comedic timing, but, until *Gypsy*, she was not known for her acting skills. Laurents, the writer, not Robbins, the director, sat her down at Sardi's restaurant and asked whether, at last, she was willing to tackle a role that required far more than had ever been asked of her before on stage or screen. According to Merman's own autobiography, he said to her, "This woman's a monster. How far are you willing to go?" She replied, "As far as you want me to…nobody's ever given me the chance before."

So now *Gypsy* had a book writer, a director, and a star but no score. Merrick and Hayward approached Cole Porter, who was too sick, Irving Berlin, who didn't like the book, and Cy Coleman and Carolyn Leigh. None of them saluted when it was run up the flagpole for them. Jerry Robbins was in favour of offering it to Stephen Sondheim with whom he had worked on *West Side Story* but Ethel Merman wouldn't hear of putting her new show in the hands of such a young and inexperienced composer. She was comfortable with Sondheim writing the lyrics but she insisted that the music be re-offered to Jule Styne. This time, he wanted it. Badly. Laurents was sceptical, "I'd never met him… I knew that Jule wrote great 'tunes' but this was a dramatic piece and I didn't know if he was capable of turning out a dramatic score." Styne offered to audition for him, a humble and unheard of act for a man in his position in the Broadway theatre and one afternoon at Robbins' apartment this experienced composer played his songs for Laurents without any appearance of resentment. Laurents loved them.

Sondheim was heartbroken. He had come so near to being allowed to write his own music for a major Broadway show and, once more, he was being offered lyrics only. Again, as with *West Side Story,* it was Oscar Hammerstein to the rescue. "Oscar persuaded me that…it was a chance to write in a whole new vein and for a star." But he was bitterly disappointed. Nobody could have predicted from such a start that Sondheim and Styne would become a happy, healthy and entirely satisfying partnership nor that together they would produce one of the greatest scores ever written for the musical theatre.

The two of them decided to wait for Laurents' storyline to give them the lead. With Laurents, they would talk through ideas and then he would write the dialogue. As soon as they knew what was happening in a scene, they could write a song for it. Sondheim needed the outline to replicate Laurents' diction and style in his lyrics, Styne needed the lyric to know what direction to take in the music. Or they did it the other way around, with Styne's music playing off Laurents' outline and Sondheim's lyrics being fired by Styne's melody. Laurents and Sondheim talked every day, at least twice. The overriding concern was to ensure that character was enhanced and reinforced through the songs with the story being driven by the score.

Laurents' storyline and dialogue were entirely clear. Two scared little girls, pushed by an overbearing mother, being dragged all over the US in pursuit of a dream that satisfied neither of them. Like most little girls, they want a home, a family, pets, a regular life. It is Rose who dreams of fame and stardom, not for them but for herself. She is, as Laurents told Merman, a monster but a monster with looks and charm which both attract and repel. Alongside the story of the two children is Rose's story, of Herbie, a nice man who wants to marry Rose but who she will eventually ruthlessly reject in order to pursue her dream of the big time.

Mark Steyn, in his entertaining *Broadway Babies Say Goodnight*, describes the opening of *Gypsy* and, in so doing, explains just what it is that makes this show explode all the conventions: "*Gypsy* begins with Uncle Jocko's Kiddie Show in Seattle: the stage is filled with grotesque moppets in tacky, home-made costumes. Suddenly, from the back of the auditorium, a rasping voice shouts, 'Sing out, Louise!', and barging her way down the aisle comes the ultimate stage mother,

Mama Rose. This is an inspired opening: effectively, the principal character hijacks her own show and disrupts the opening number." It is illuminating, at least to me, that Steyn, a recognised expert on the musical theatre, regards *Gypsy* as "the greatest of all musicals" without being able to define whether it is, in fact, a musical comedy or a musical play. It is, he says, "dramatically indestructible, but musically appealing enough to have produced more cast recordings than any other show."

In Rose's ambition is the drive of an entire nation in which anybody can become President, anyone can be a star, you just have to want it badly enough. Overarching the personal stories is the story of a restless America, the relentless and constantly moving society in which, if you are not moving up, you are sinking down. Rose is the American dream manqué, the grotesque side of a people who believe that they are their own destiny and that hard work will make its own opportunities. She is also the flip side of good parenting, the nightmare of any mother who suspects she might be demanding too much of her children. The mother myth, the idea that every mother loves her children more than her own life, that she will sacrifice everything for their welfare, and that all she desires for her own life is that they be happy and healthy, is, in *Gypsy*, exploded.

At the end, when it becomes clear that Gypsy no longer needs nor wants the constant interference of her mother, when she finally tells her what she has done to her life and that of her sister, when she destroys Rose's belief in the rightness of her own causes, Rose's frustration and fears become manifest and public in one of the most remarkable sequences on the musical stage, the sung nervous breakdown that is 'Rose's Turn'. This is a mad scene on a par with *Lucia di Lammermoor*. It is operatic in structure and is a sustained acting and singing *tour de force* lasting more than five minutes.

In 'Rose's Turn', Rose tries to put into words her life's work, what she feels she has done and made of her children, to defend herself against Gypsy's accusations, to explain herself. Sondheim wanted it to finish on a note of real madness, a scratchy violin sound fading on her last softly delivered words – "For me, for meee, for meee, for m…" but Merman wanted a real finish and, when Hammerstein came to see a run-through, he agreed with her. After that, he told Sondheim, "The audience is so anxious to applaud her that they are not listening to the scene that follows. Since the scene that follows is what the entire play is about, if you want them to listen, you must let them release themselves."

While Laurents, Styne and Sondheim, together with their designers, Jo Mielziner and the eccentric Pène du Bois, were happily working on the show as a united team, Jerome Robbins was feeling left out. Whereas with *West Side Story* he had had complete artistic control to choreograph and direct, and even, because it had been his idea, to nudge the music, lyrics, and book in the direction he thought they should take, with *Gypsy*, he was forced to direct what the rest of the team were giving him. A choreographer by training and predilection, he always directed with a visual and physical bias. Here, the words and music were driving the show and he felt his role was diminished. "It's a book show," he kept saying to Laurents, "your show, not mine."

From the beginning, he had had a different vision of the show from his collaborators. He wanted it to be a tribute to American vaudeville, wrote William Emmet Long in his *Broadway, the Golden Years*, "He went ahead, without consulting his collaborators, engaging the services of trapeze artists, jugglers, old strippers, comedians, and animal acts." "Jerry saw it as a great panorama of a show," commented Arthur Laurents, "…Actually, *Gypsy* is a show about three people." Clearly, without an agreed basis for what the show was to be, it is hardly surprising that Robbins' nose was firmly out of joint almost from the beginning and a lot of performers who had been hired had to be fired even before they got to the rehearsal stage.

For some reason the producer, David Merrick, took against it too and well before opening night was saying to anyone who would listen, about his own show, "It's terrible. I want to get rid of this show." When Jack Klugman, an experienced and popular actor who was playing Herbie, wanted to invest in the show, Merrick said, "You don't want to invest in this show. It's going to be a bomb." Leland Hayward and Jule Styne, overhearing this conversation, took out their chequebooks and asked Merrick how much it would take to buy him out. He stopped running the show down after that.

Another nasty row took place just before the Philadelphia pre-Broadway opening when Jule Styne completed his overture. Theatre buffs now argue vociferously about which is the greatest show overture ever written. The two that invariably win are Bernstein's *Candide* and Styne's *Gypsy* but on the day when Styne's chosen conductor, Milton Rosenstock, first played it for Robbins and the rest of the 'creatives', Merrick and Robbins hated it. They agreed that it might be left in place until after the Philadelphia opening so it could be tried out in front of an audience. Robbins was implacable. "If it doesn't go, we do the choruses. All right?" (The standard overture contains the choruses of the songs to be sung in that act of the show). "Not all right with me," Styne replied, furious, "We open with this goddamn overture. I'll not cut one note of it." We don't know what would have happened if that Philly audience hadn't liked it because, when the famous trumpet notes signifying the strippers sounded, the audience began to cheer and applaud, unheard of for an overture.

The next skirmish between the two colleagues was when Robbins cut 'Little Lamb', an important character song for Louise, without so much as informing Styne. Styne, a little man with a lot of dignity, walked up onstage and announced, "Mr Robbins, I have notified my lawyers in New York that I am withdrawing the entire score unless 'Little Lamb' is put back in tonight." Back in went the song.

Robbins had an argument with just about everybody on *Gypsy*. He had staged a scene where the two little girls eavesdrop on Rose and Herbie from atop a piece of scenery high above the stage. The actress playing June, Jaqueline Mayro, was, as Robbins knew, afraid of heights and, rather than restage the scene, he cut her song.

But the last rumble was with Jule Styne who knew how to take care of himself. The orchestra pit at New York's Winter Garden Theatre was much lower than the other theatres the show had played on its pre-New York tour. Styne, concerned that the music was sounding muffled, asked Robbins for some platforms to raise the level of the players. He promised but didn't deliver. When the official opening night in New York rolled around Styne wandered into the auditorium in the afternoon and, noticing that the pit had not been raised, took Robbins by the neck, "Jerry, I know you're responsible for those orchestra platforms not being here…I am going to throw you into the pit. When you yell, no one will hear you. Just like nobody will hear my music." Robbins blamed the producers, the producers blamed the stagehands, and everybody except Jule went home to change. But Jule Styne was not without resources. A friend with a furniture warehouse came in to rescue the situation and by curtaintime the orchestra were a foot and a half taller than they had been that afternoon. "See?" said Robbins to Styne at intermission, "the music is clearly audible." "Yes, baby," said Styne, "that's 'cause they're all sitting on barstools."

*Gypsy* opened on May 21st 1959 and it seemed that everyone in New York who was anyone in the theatre and music was there. Richard Rodgers, Alan Jay Lerner, Irving Berlin, Leonard Bernstein, Mary Martin, Truman Capote, and all the film crowd came to wonder and stayed to cheer. The reviews in the morning papers would be sensational, especially for Ethel Merman. Walter Kerr, who came a few days later, wrote, "Miss Merman seems to have piled all her past successes together and to be standing on top of them." Kenneth Tynan in *The New Yorker* went further, as usual, "The first act brings together in effortless coalition all the arts of the American musical stage at the highest point in their development. So smooth is the blending of skills, so precise the interlocking of songs, speech, and dance, that the sheer contemplation of techniques becomes a thrilling emotional experience. It is like being present at the triumphant solution of some harsh architectural problem, stone after massive stone is nudged and juggled into place, with a balance so nice that the finished structure seems as light as an exhalation, though in fact it is earthquake-proof."

Last word goes to the lady herself, Gypsy Rose Lee, who walked slowly down the aisle to her seat at the Broadway opening with her son Erik Lee Preminger as her date, wearing a simple but devastating white silk blouse and long black taffeta skirt on her still perfect figure and putting to shame all the overdressed and bejewelled New York matrons who surrounded her, "I never played myself or even my own mother in *Gypsy*, but I played another part closer to myself, darling. It was far from Broadway, someplace in Ohio. I starred as *Auntie Mame*. That part was much more me."

I always hope she was joking. Because if *Gypsy*, book, show, and later movie, was a fable, so was the life of Gypsy Rose Lee. And if anyone paid a high price for living someone else's American dream, it was little Louise Hovick.

# 8. *"Miracle of Miracles"*

O N A COLD night in 1967, I took my father, Samuel Leon, to see the first London production of *Fiddler on the Roof*, starring Topol as Tevye. As he settled himself in his stalls seat and fussed with his programme and coat he happened to glance towards the stage where, unusually for its time, the heavy stage curtains were not drawn and the set was therefore displayed. "That," said Sammy, with his usual confidence, pointing at the stage, "is where I was born." "No, darling," I said, patronisingly, "that's a fictional place, designed by the great Boris Aronson, called Anatevka, not Aleksandrov where you come from. It's a stage set, it's not real." He gave me the Look, the one with which all parents can quell all children, and stopped folding his coat. He glared at me. "I know that," he said, with great dignity, "do you think I'm an idiot? I know it's a stage set, I'm sitting in a theatre, aren't I? But that Boris Aronson, he must have been born in Aleksandrov, because that there is where I was born. Would you get me an ice-cream, please? Strawberry, if they have it." I settled back into my place, in both senses of the word.

Before a single note had been played by that damn Fiddler, Sammy had identified what matters most about *Fiddler* and instantly recognised its affinity with his own life. Not only had he been born in a *shtetl* like Anatevka (a rural Eastern European village inhabited only by Jews), in Bock and Harnick's great musical, adapted from the short stories of Sholem Aleichem, their leading character, Tevye, was a milkman. Although his father, my grandfather, was a tailor, his mother, my grandmother, was a milkman, er, woman. So had there been a single false note or phony emotion or incorrect fact in *Fiddler*, Sammy would have found it. But he didn't because he couldn't; *Fiddler*, along with all the other great musicals, may not be real but it is true and its truth ranges further than the specifics of its setting and time.

*Fiddler on the Roof* is perfect because its values reflect the joys and fears of parents everywhere. Will the children be happy? Will they be safe? Will they know love and comfort? Will they remember who they are and where they come from? Like Lorraine Hansberry's signature play, *A Raisin in the Sun*, about a black family in the Chicago ghetto of 1959, it couldn't be more specific about its origins and intent. That family is black, Tevye's family is Jewish, both are defined by their ethnicity, both are concerned with conflict of tradition and the lengths to which their young can stray without losing it. Jerome Robbins, the show's original director and choreographer always said that *Fiddler* is not just about Tevye finding suitable husbands for his daughters. That, he said, is what *happens* in the show. What it's *about* is the passing of a way of life.

It is not an accident that the show opens with a song and dance called 'Tradition'. This is the bedrock of the musical or, more accurately, the play with songs. Against a background of pogroms and unrest in the Russian hinterlands, the constant threat of eviction or death, the struggle for survival in a cold mean world, Tevye's five daughters must find husbands. The young men must be Jewish, they must be willing to take a poor girl without a dowry, they must be able to look after her in the times of trouble that are surely coming from the Tsar, from the Cossacks, and from anyone who doesn't like Jews, which is everyone who isn't Jewish. If you're a milkman and the horse goes lame, well, you have to pull the cart yourself. Life is hard. The girls must find husbands, with or without the help of the matchmaker.

Tevye's wife, Golde, has to put food on the table for a family of seven and has no time to reflect on whether she is happy or not. "Do I love you? I suppose I do," she sings, and he sings back, "And I suppose I love you too." Her life is bounded by her religion, her husband, her daughters, her wooden cabin, and, in these dangerous times, the need to find suitable husbands for her daughters. So what would happen if her three oldest daughters were to choose their own? Unthinkable. And, when it happens, she, in the manner of women everywhere, is the first to find compromises.

The last scene is the one that really speaks to the quality of this musical more than any other. It is when the Tsar has issued an order that all Jews must leave the country in three days and the family is breaking up, going in different directions, some to America, some to Poland, some to Siberia. They sing of Anatevka, "tumble-down, workaday Anatevka," knowing not just that they are leaving the only home they have ever known but also that the traditions that have held them together for generations must now be regenerated in places they have never seen, among strangers, and that they may never see one another again. There are no mobile telephones or instant messaging; there is just the love that binds them and the traditions that have sustained them. Will it be enough?

That these are wonderful songs we now take for granted, that there is not one wasted musical moment, not one song you can't, with a few moments' reflection, sing yourself, is a prerequisite of a perfect musical. But can you think of a single musical written in this century about which you say that there isn't a single song that doesn't *have* to be there for sense, for emotion, for plot, or for character? Me neither.

Ethan Mordden, the theatre historian, writes that Aronson's designs are less about the literal village of Anatevka, with their liberal borrowing from the paintings of Chagall, and more about who the people are who live there. "Aronson seemed almost to move a camera from one part of the village to another. This is what a culture looks like".

Thelma Ruby, who took over from Miriam Karlin in that original London production and subsequently played Golde all over the world, told me of a Japanese matron who came back-stage to see her in Tokyo. She bowed to Thelma, smiled shyly, and said in her halting English, "Thank you for performance. Beautiful. But, tell me please, how you know so much about Japanese family?" In an echo of her query came one from the Japanese producer to Joseph Stein, who wrote *Fiddler*'s book, "Tell me, do they understand this show in America? It's so Japanese."

Yes, they understand it in America. And in Paris, in Rome, in Helsinki and in Sydney. They understand it wher-ever parents have children and wherever children grow up to discover they don't necessarily want what their parents want for them. They understand it whenever the future clashes with the past and wherever tradition and modernity meet. *Fiddler on the Roof*, as culturally specific as a Negro Spiritual, is, like a Negro Spiritual, universal and all-encompassing.

My father understood that. So did his mother, which is why she pushed a cart clear across a continent, carrying two small children, one a babe in arms, to get to a better place where they didn't have to be afraid, where they could grow up to sit comfortably in the stalls at Her Majesty's Theatre, Haymarket and eat a strawberry ice-cream.

# 9. Being Alive

ONE EVENING, SEVERAL years ago, I was sitting with my friend, Lynn Redgrave, in the Watergate Restaurant in Washington DC. Lynn was starring in *Company* next door at the Kennedy Centre as part of a madly successful series of revivals of Sondheim's musicals for which audiences had come from all over the country and the world. The restaurant was heaving. The other diners were elegantly attired and excited to have nabbed, first a ticket, then a table for this most desirable of all events. There was not a spare table or even a spare chair except for one at our table.

Across the room I saw a compact grey-haired man with a trim beard, in jeans and a dark green t-shirt, standing completely still amid all the hubbub, and I knew that almost nobody in this crowded restaurant had any idea that the reason for all this excitement, Stephen Sondheim himself, was standing amongst them, unrecognised. They were all there because of him but he was known to them only through his shows. As he sat down, he said to Lynn and me, "We should have gone somewhere quieter."

In choosing shows for this book I had to weigh a number of criteria but eventually, the mists cleared and it became obvious which should be included and which, however reluctantly, would have to wait for next time. Until now. What do you decide to write about when you're writing about the work of Stephen Sondheim? "*Sweeney Todd,*" said the first friend I asked, "no contest." "*Company,*" said a fellow theatre writer, "how could you ignore that?" "*Assassins,*" insisted a third, "No, *"Passion."* "No, *Pacific Overtures."* "How could you say that? Have you forgotten *A Little Night Music*?" "Well, no, but the prize surely goes to *Follies*?" And so on. Privately, I was determined to focus on my personal favourite *Sunday in the Park wih George*, a show that shows the rest of us what it's actually like to be an artist, to make art.

"Every time Steve writes a new show, Broadway gets reinvented." I don't know exactly who said that but I've heard it attributed to Hal Prince, Bernadette Peters, Ned Sherrin, Sheridan Morley, and several others. Whoever said it, it's true. What's more, our one and only living musical theatre genius is the direct descendent of all the other great show-makers in this book but of one in particular.

The line is clear as a newly polished diamond. The libretto for *Showboat* was written in 1927 by a young lyricist, Oscar Hammerstein II. He became the partner of composer Richard Rodgers and together they cut the patterns that formed the musical theatre of the 20th century.

While they were at it, writing nine musicals with titles such as *Oklahoma!, Carousel,* and *South Pacific,* a boy with an unhappy family background became friends with Hammerstein's son,

Jamie. Soon, the boys were inseparable and the teenager was spending more time in the Hammerstein house than he was in his own. He begged Oscar to teach him how to write a show. He brought him his first effort at writing a full-length musical, *By George*, a parody of life at his exclusive school, the George School in Bucks County, Pennsylvania, expecting that Hammerstein would immediately produce it on Broadway. Instead of patting the boy on the head and sending him away with a smile, he treated him as he would a professional.

He said to him, "Now, do you want my opinion as though I didn't know you? Well, it's the worst thing I've ever read." The boy's face fell, "I didn't say it was untalented, I said it was terrible. And if you want to know *why* it's terrible, I'll tell you." He deconstructed the show, indicating where he had taken the wrong approach, where his lyrics didn't fit his music, where his music wasn't suitable for their place in the plot and generally giving him a master class on the art of musical writing. Upset but not discouraged, the boy kept coming back, asking for more. Over the course of a number of years, until he went away to college, he received the most important lessons of his life from a master teacher who took the time to impart to an unhappy boy what he would need to make a life in the theatre.

For Stephen Sondheim, Oscar Hammerstein was teacher, mentor, and surrogate father, the most important figure in his professional life. Until his death in 1960, he guided and directed, cajoled and coaxed, showing the way. When Sondheim wanted to turn down playwright Arthur Laurents' invitation to write lyrics for *West Side Story*, because he wanted to write music as well as words, it was Hammerstein who persuaded him that the experience of working with such professionals as Laurents, composer Leonard Bernstein, and director/choreographer Jerome Robbins would outweigh any ambition to be an independent songwriter in his own right.

He did it again when, although Sondheim had been touted by Robbins as composer/lyricist for *Gypsy*, the star, Ethel Merman, flatly refused to allow the young composer to write her music, insisting instead on the more experienced Jule Styne. Sondheim would have walked away, except that Hammerstein pointed out that he had never written for a star and that Styne would teach him much that he didn't know about shaping a show around a personality. Without Hammerstein, then, two of the shows which are so important to the history of the musical theatre that we have included them in this book of perfect musicals, would have been very different and, possibly, not nearly as good.

For the rest of Hammerstein's life, Sondheim never did anything without consulting him. When he knew he was dying, Oscar asked Steve if, as a favour to him, he would offer to work with Rodgers as his lyricist. Sondheim wasn't enthusiastic. Rodgers was a difficult man. Where Hammerstein was happily married, always smiling, full of wisdom and laughter, Rodgers was a womaniser, a jealous, unforgiving man with a mean streak. But, in a lifetime, Hammerstein had asked Sondheim for nothing and given so much. Despite his determination never again to write lyrics without also composing the music, Sondheim agreed, and the result, after Hammerstein's death, was the beautiful score for *Do I Hear A Waltz?* But the pair were a mismatch and this was their only joint project.

It is impossible to overestimate Hammerstein's importance in Sondheim's life. When he died, Sondheim was bereft. Already 40, he had yet to have a show of his own produced on Broadway. But he had already been associated with Leonard Bernstein, Arthur Laurents, Jerome Robbins, Jule Styne, and his best friend, producer Hal Prince, in ground-breaking shows. And then, in 1962, came *A Funny Thing Happened on the Way to the Forum,* a jokey, patchy, and brilliant musical written with Burt Shevelove and Larry Gelbart, based on the stories of the Roman playwright, Plautus. If you looked carefully, as Sondheim realised only when the show was already on the road, Sondheim's elegant and beautifully crafted songs were completely at odds with Shevelove and Gelbart's hysterically funny but madcap book. A lesson learned about working with others, as Sondheim said about *Forum,* "Make sure you and your collaborators are writing the same show."

It wasn't, though, until *Company* in 1970, that we begin to see the scope of the immense talent of a man who simply saw the world differently than anyone ever had before and was able to make us see it theatrically through his eyes. He isn't afraid of the word 'art' but Sondheim is, above all, a man of the theatre. He doesn't write songs unless he knows the context. Give him a character, a situation, a plotline, and he'll write a song that will break your heart, make you fall off your seat with laughter, and give you something to think about, often all at the same time. Remove the theatrical context and he's paralysed.

*Company,* written with George Furth, is about marriage and commitment. Or the lack of it. Bobby is single. His friends, five couples of different ages and temperaments, are all married or, at any rate, together. They sing of what it means to be in love, or to fall out of love, of weddings, of divorce, of boredom, of loneliness, and the rewards and drawbacks of allowing anyone to come too close. While Bobby struggles with his single state, his friends (like Sondheim's) are, despite their own unhappy relationships, forever trying to talk or sing him out of it. *Company,* Sondheim's first masterwork, is completely original. Its characters are chic, sophisticated, educated, self-aware, uncertain Manhattanites and instantly recognisable to anyone who has ever lived in New York. The songs cut to the quick as no musical has ever done before and the audience actually winces as some of the lyrics hit their marks.

The form of the show is deceptively simple and it is only as you hear the songs again that you realise how precisely they fit into a pattern of relationships. It is a man – Sondheim himself? – trying on a number of templates for living and wondering how they might fit. It is so clever that at first you might mistake it for an exercise, albeit a very successful one. *Company* was where the unshakeable soubriquet "Too clever by half," was first attached to his work, "All head, no heart." But it's not that, it's that the heart and the emotions are lingering just below the surface, trying not to be subsumed by the thoughts and contradictions of the brain.

"*Company* says very clearly that to be emotionally committed to somebody is very difficult, but to be alone is impossible," in Sondheim's own description. *Company* is where you first notice that Sondheim's musical language is inextricably tied to his lyrical vocabulary and that there is not a syllable that doesn't fit onto precisely the right note nor a note that doesn't make a lyrical statement. His songs, in common with every true work of art, reward repeated attention.

Those who complain that they can't sing any Sondheim song except 'Send In The Clowns' have never taken a Sondheim show CD with them on a long car journey. Like Rembrandt's *The Night Watch*, or Shakespeare's *Macbeth*, every time you engage with it you notice something you've never noticed before and want to examine further. And, once you get the hang of the melodies, when you listen to them more than once, they're eminently singable as every great cabaret and jazz performer from Barbara Cook to Cleo Laine will tell you. As Richard Rodgers himself once said, "The tunes you come out humming are the same as the tunes you went in humming."

Sondheim's tunes are different. They reward attention and care, like everything else worth having.

*Company*, in 1970, was followed the following year by something entirely different. Sondheim saw a photograph in the *New York Times*, showing Gloria Swanson standing in the wreckage of the old Roxy Theatre which was being demolished. At almost the same time there was a small item in the newspaper about a reunion of former *Ziegfeld Follies* showgirls, in their day the most glamorous girls in New York. The result was *Follies,* a nostalgic look back to vaudeville and the turn of the century entertainments of beautiful girls wearing bubbles, feathers, sequins…and very little else. Two couples – two of the showgirls and their stage-door johnnies, now husbands – come to say goodbye to the theatre of their youth before it is demolished and revisit their younger selves, to discover what they have made of their lives, of the promise of those more innocent days.

Like *Company, Follies* is about unhappy marriages, the reality of the present in the light of the dreams of the past, but this time Sondheim, his co-writer James Goldman, and his director, Hal Prince, had made the marriages a kind of metaphor for a transitional world, the death of one kind of musical theatre, the emergence of something more modern, more edgy, and for this the old theatre – the building and, by extension, the artform itself – physically had to die.

The reviews for *Follies*, like those for *Company*, were, for the most part, tepid, although the most perceptive of the critics, while not much liking the subject matter, at least acknowledged its innovation and the shock of the new. T.E. Kalem, of *Time Magazine*, realised that these two shows had changed the landscape, "The frontier of the American musical theatre is wherever Harold Prince and Stephen Sondheim are." While not classified a hit in the sense of recouping its investors' money, it ran for more than 500 performances and won seven Tony Awards. Audiences found it a difficult show but they understood that, in its mourning of the passing of the era of the Roxy and the *Ziegfeld* girls, it was also saying goodbye to the era of Porter, Gershwin, Berlin, and the entire musical theatre life of the first half of the century.

*A Little Night Music* (1973) is based on the Ingmar Bergman film *Smiles of a Summer Night* in an adaptation by Hugh Wheeler. This time, Sondheim wanted to write a period piece, but one with fantastical elements, similar to a Jean Anouilh play or even Shakespeare's *A Midsummer Night's Dream*. He wanted "whipped cream with knives," a heightened atmosphere in which characters come together in a country house for the weekend and fall in love with all the wrong people and have to find their way out of the maze. The Bergman movie, with its middle-aged actress finally deciding to settle down with her favourite lover only to discover that he has married an 18-year-old, fitted the bill perfectly and Sondheim's songs, all in waltz-time, are, with one exception, inextricably bound to the plot moment from which they spring.

That exception is, of course, 'Send In The Clowns', Sondheim's only chart hit. Prince and Sondheim had cast the diminutive Glynis Johns as the actress Desirée Armfeldt opposite Broadway leading man Len Cariou but, although he had several comic numbers, by the time the show was ready to open in Boston, he still didn't have his own romantic song. Sondheim, as always when his shows were out of town, was still agonising over the songs not yet written. He was working all night to complete the score, and all day to rehearse it with the arranger, the singers, the orchestra, the music director. Then pretty Glynis Johns, not wanting to make a fuss, pointed out that, although she was the leading lady, she didn't have a song at all. Sondheim had done this deliberately, assuming that she was a non-singing actress who would not want to be burdened with having to sing his difficult music, which was almost true except that what he didn't know was that she had a sweet, light singing voice which was perfectly serviceable with the right song.

Sondheim went away to write a song for Cariou but came in the next morning with a song for Johns. Taking all the technical restrictions into consideration, it had short, clipped lines to allow her to breathe easily and the range – the distance between the highest and the lowest note – is deliberately narrow. Cariou, professional that he is, laughed and accepted the situation; Johns, professional that *she* is, learned the song that day and put it into the show that night. It is conventional wisdom these days to consider 'Send In The Clowns' to be hackneyed but that is just sophistry. Its lyric can still break your heart. A woman who has everything she thought she wanted now knows that the one thing that is indispensible to her happiness is forever out of her reach.

Out of reach indeed was the next Sondheim musical. Steve had to be dragged kicking and screaming into this one but his best friend, closest collaborator, and regular director, Hal Prince, had fallen in love with a play by John Weidman about, of all things, the visit of Commodore Perry to 19th century Japan, then a closed feudal society, where his mission was to make a treaty between the two unlikely trading partners. Prince asked Sondheim to write the music but he had no interest in Japanese culture or music and couldn't see a way into it until he realised that the Japanese scale had some relationship to the Spanish, particularly Manuel de Falla.

Prince's idea was bold: instead of the *King and I* approach to the Orient, where the exotic was seen through the eyes of Mrs Anna, an Englishwoman, here he decided that the point of view should be Japanese with the exotic being provided by the oddity of the foreigners, the Americans, crashing into their closed culture. Inevitably, Sondheim became intrigued, then fascinated. This show contains the song that has always seemed dearest to his heart, 'Someone In A Tree', where a 10-year-old boy up a tree outside the room where the treaty is being signed overhears the debate and reports on it without understanding what he is hearing, just as Sondheim, at the same age, had to observe his parents' divorce without understanding its consequences.

*Pacific Overtures* didn't really work as a Broadway musical, having no central characters with whom the audience could identify and being too concerned with politics over plot but the idea of a show which tackles the conflict between an ancient society forever looking backward towards its history and a modern one looking towards the future, through the eyes of the older civilisation, continues to fascinate.

On a trip to London, Sondheim, always interested in melodrama ("farce and melodrama have always been my favourite forms of theatre"), saw Christopher Bond's play about *Sweeney Todd: The Demon Barber of Fleet Street*, an entirely fictional character who has somehow become so inextricably part of English folklore that he has a tangible presence as an historical murderer. Steve loved it. He wanted to write a Grand Guignol opera and that's exactly, with writer Hugh Wheeler, what he did. His anti-hero, Sweeney Todd, has been wrongly imprisoned and transported. When he returns to London, he discovers that the Judge who sentenced him has raped his wife and adopted his daughter so he swears revenge. He takes lodgings above a pie-shop owned by Mrs Lovett ('The Worst Pies in London') and sets up again as a barber. When he fails to kill the Judge, he embarks on a killing spree. His barber's chair has a cunning spring which sends his victims into the cellar where Mrs Lovett, reluctant to waste meat, simply bakes their flesh into her pies ('Try The Priest').

*Sweeney Todd* is a huge show. Whereas *Pacific Overtures* was much improved in its second New York outing by being given a smaller production, *Sweeney Todd* can only be done properly on a gigantic scale. Initially, according to Meryle Secrest's masterful biography, *Stephen Sondheim: A Life*, Steve wanted a less elaborate production than Hal Prince gave it, "I meant it to be done as a small piece because I wanted to just scare people," but having seen it several times on both sides of the Atlantic, I find it difficult to imagine it as simply a scary little show.

It has an operatic score with leit-motifs for each character, growing out of plot and emotion. The intimate and bloody story of Sweeney Todd and Mrs Lovett is set against the background of the dehumanising Industrial Revolution in London, a large chorus illustrating the plight of ordinary people as they struggle to live in an increasingly heartless society.

This is Victorian London as Dickens saw it but it is also revenge through the eyes of a supremely clever and sensitive man who was once a damaged small boy. Stephen Sondheim, abandoned by his father at the age of ten, the son of a manipulative and vicious mother who used and abused him, found in *Sweeney Todd* the means to get back at all those who had hurt and injured him when he was a helpless child. Listen to the lyrics he gives to Johanna who, like her little bird, just wants to be free and you can hear a child begging for help. Listen to those he gives the Judge, an incestuous parent, and you can hear the anger of a grown-up child desperate for acceptance. Listen to Todd's lyrics and the cry for vengeance becomes undeniable. It is very powerful.

The first production starred Len Cariou as Todd and Angela Lansbury as the irrepressibly amoral Mrs Lovett. Despite many technical and staging difficulties, the critics raved about *Sweeney Todd* and it won eight Tonys, including Best Musical. And Jule Styne, one of the composers whom Sondheim most admired told him, as quoted in Secrest's book, "I think the most unbelievable job of music-writing, and I say this with deep reverence and envy...is *Sweeney Todd.*" For Sondheim, in Hammerstein's absence, this is perhaps the best compliment of all.

One of my favourite Sondheim scores is the one he wrote for a flop. *Merrily We Roll Along,* based on a 1934 play by Kaufman and Hart, is a classic example of Sondheim's own stricture to be sure you're working on the same show as your collaborators. Played backwards, *Merrily* tells the sad story of three best friends – a composer, a lyricist, a novelist – who start as bright-eyed adolescents with all the hopes and ambitions of the talented young, and who succeed professionally but lose, along the path to success, all their youthful commitment, their integrity, and their friendship and become, in two out of three cases, burned-out, cynical, and unattractive.

The book didn't work. The show started by showing the former friends as they would become. Nobody wanted to see young actors dressed up as older people, pretending to be jerks. Prince admitted that in the end he had no idea how to stage *Merrily* and lacked the courage of his convictions, which were initially to mount it very simply in rehearsal clothes without a set. But the songs are marvellous. Sondheim was at the top of his game and nobody did it better. You can extract any lyric from this show and speak it, it will make sense as conversation. The music is colourful and charming. I'm grieved that these great songs are so rarely heard because the show is virtually unproduceable. If you cast young actors, they can't manage the beginning of the show, where they have to be jaded and cynical; if you cast older actors, they are not believable as kids at the end.

A completely unforeseen fallout from the failure of *Merrily We Roll Along* was that the bad reviews and unrelenting criticism of that production triggered the breakup of the partnership between Hal Prince and Stephen Sondheim, a partnership closer than friendship, closer than brothers. They agree that it was Hal who wanted to look for new collaborators but both claim not to be sure why. Hal was particularly depressed after the split and he followed *Merrily* with a string of flops which didn't help his mood. Sondheim, though, always the pessimist in the duo, turned out to be more resilient. He was looking for another collaborator and another project.

Which brings us to my own favourite of all his works, *Sunday in the Park with George*. Sondheim met a young playwright, James Lapine, and, because Lapine was both a photographer and a designer as well as a writer, they were looking at visual images for inspiration. Lapine suggested Georges Seurat's curious painting, *A Sunday Afternoon on the Island of La Grande Jatte*. They noticed that, despite there being many characters in the painting, none of them were looking at one another and Lapine pointed out that the one person missing was the painter himself. They became interested in Seurat's life, his relationship to his mistress and to his mother, how he approached his art. He, more than any other artist, had developed pointilism, a way of putting paint onto canvas without mixing it first so that putting blue and yellow very close to one another in tiny points of paint would provide the eye with the impression of bright green.

While he denies it, this show is about Sondheim himself as an artist, about the act of creation, about making something that only you know how to make. My favourite line from all of Sondheim's shows is from his song 'Finishing The Hat', "Look, I made a hat, where there never was a hat." It is the justification of all the effort and thought, of all the anxiety and feeling, of all the pain and uncertainty of creating a work of art. You just have to finish the hat. If you ignore the woman you love, if you forget your family, if you yell at your children, it matters, but not as much as finishing the hat.

In *Sunday*, all Sondheim's preoccupations from most of his other shows reach fruition. Art, primarily, but also children, kindness, work, loneliness, friendship, the relationship between the past and the future, making rather than destroying, and the conflict between commercialism and purity. As we learn about each of the characters in the painting, we also learn what their dreams are and how they see their place in the world. And beyond it.

Sondheim wrote, early in the writing process, "The show is, in part, about how creation takes on a life of its own, how artists feed off art (we off Seurat); the artist's relationship to his material." He used repeated images – 'colour', 'light', 'connect', 'order' – to indicate Seurat's and indeed his own relationship to his art. The overall theme is that art is inevitable, even when it isolates the artist from his own life, a tragic and, at the same time, realistic view of Sondheim himself. The Tony Awards that year almost ignored *Sunday in the Park with George,* winning awards only for its sets and lighting, which shocked all of us who thought it was perhaps the best show ever. Later that year, though, it won the Pulitzer Prize for Drama, the most prestigious award in the field and only the 6th musical to have been so honoured.

It would be tempting to make this book all about Sondheim or to analyse each moment of each show, but what we're looking at here is what makes the great shows universal, not just his. If *Into The Woods* (1987) is about conquering fear and being careful what you wish for, and *Assassins* (1990) his thoughts on politicians and the American dream, and *Passion* (1994) is his most heartfelt meditation on love, it is clear that there is no part of his oeuvre that *doesn't* address something deeply personal in us all.

Stephen Sondheim is, as Sheridan Morley once wrote, "the greatest lyric poet of contemporary world theatre." But let's not forget that Oscar Hammerstein ii was Sondheim's spiritual father. Frank Rich wrote that Sondheim, the logical heir to the American musical theatre tradition, had "changed the texture of the musical as radically as Hammerstein once did in *Show Boat* and *Oklahoma!* – but, even more than Hammerstein did, he has built a bridge between the musical and the more daring playwriting of his time." Both Hammerstein and Sondheim would, I believe be more than satisfied with that.

And looking toward the future of the musical theatre, so can we.